RISK AND THE BUSINESS ENVIRONMENT

by

Alan Gordon

OTHER BOOKS IN THE SERIES

Business Finance for Risk Management

Corporate Risk Management

Liability Exposures

Physical Control of Risk

Risk Analysis

Risk Financing

British Library Cataloguing in Publication Data

Gordon, Alan
Risk and the business environment — 2nd ed
I. Title
658.403

ISBN 1856090345

RISK AND THE BUSINESS ENVIRONMENT

by
Alan Gordon

LONDON

WITHERBY & Co. Ltd.
32-36 Aylesbury Street
London EC1R 0ET

Published for
The Institute of Risk Management

First Edition 1987
Second Edition 1992

ISBN 1 85609 034 5

Printed and Published by

Witherby & Co. Ltd.
32-36 Aylesbury Street
London EC1R 0ET

Tel: 071-251 5341
Fax: 071-251 1296

Preface

In a world of change risk is ever present. As the rate of change and the level of complexity increases, the need to control the risks that emerge becomes greater. This has been acknowledged in recent years with the development of the discipline of risk management.

This book is aimed therefore at students of risk management, and particularly, but not exclusively, those studying for the examinations of the Institute of Risk Management.

Study of the business environment is necessary as it is both a source of the risks which the modern business organisation has to manage and is the background to the daily practice of industrial risk management.

The text is therefore an introduction to those areas and concepts of the business environment of relevance to the risk manager. As much of the material is of an introductory nature, students are encouraged to undertake further reading from such references as 'Business Economics Made Simple' and 'Business Law Made Simple', published by Heinemann or other similar introductory texts.

Finally thanks are due to those who have contributed variously to this book. To the members of the Department of Banking and Insurance at Glasgow College of Technology and in particular Dr Gordon Dickson and John Reid for their encouragement and advice, to Alan Louth of Rowntree Mackintosh for helpful and constructive comments on the text, and to my wife and family for their support and forbearance.

Alan Gordon
Glasgow
July 1987

Acknowledgements

I am grateful to the undernoted firms and organisations for their permission to reproduce certain diagrams, tables etc. in this book.

Bank of England Quarterly Bulletin
Euromoney Publications Ltd.
W Heinemann Ltd.
Holt, Rinehart and Winston
Kluwer Publishing Ltd.
McGraw-Hill Inc.
Pitman Publishing Ltd.
Witherby & Co. Ltd.

Risk and the Business Environment

CONTENTS

Chapter One

BUSINESS ENVIRONMENT AND RISK

1.0 Introduction

Risk Management is not new. Many practising managers will claim that they have been using it to a greater or lesser extent for a long number of years. They have seen it simply as part of their job. This is because much of risk management has been described as applied common sense. This is both its strength and weakness, because to quote Neil Crockford in *An Introduction to Risk Management:*

"one man's common sense is another's novel concept while it is heresy to a third and nonsense to a fourth."

It is not new because risk is not new. Mankind has been required throughout the centuries to manage the risks with which it has been presented as they have both threatened existence and offered opportunities. Risk therefore is pervasive. The nature and the causes of the risks may change over time, the extent of the damage or reward that may result may also change but risk itself cannot be avoided. So there are grounds for arguing that "risk management" is merely a new label on old and familiar practices.

And yet the methodological approach to the management of risks advocated by its proponents is new. It involves insurance but it is more than insurance. It may be a specialised part of financial management as mentioned by Olson and Simkiss in the *Geneva Papers, April 1982* but it is more than that. It may require knowledge of chemical processes, the fundamentals of fire engineering or the physical properties of different materials but it involves more than these; and although the risk manager may draw upon statistical techniques, it is more than the analysis of loss statistics - valuable those these may be. Risk management involves a multi-disciplinary approach.

This is why production managers, personnel managers, financial managers and company secretaries, to mention only a few, could in the past claim to have been practicing risk management. However such management of risk in the past has been, by and large, on a piecemeal basis. Insurance managers, fire engineers, statisticians and the like have assiduously researched many of the aspects of risk, but no one has taken an overall view and sought to combine the efforts and the lessons of the various experts for an enhancement in the control and management of risk. Much of the practice of risk management in the business enterprise has therefore been uncoordinated. Hence the description often accorded to the role of risk management as one of coordination of the efforts to manage risk. The risk manager is thereby responsible for coordination of the action to combat all forms of risk that afflict the organisation. This therefore is the novelty of the approach to these problems described as risk management. Specific responsibility for the identification, analysis and financing of risk becomes the responsibility of a particular manager, but the persons ultimately responsible for the implementation of measures to control risk remain the line managers.

1.1 The Decision Process

The risk manager, in common with his counterparts from other areas of a business or public enterprise, is required to perform a variety of roles: policy formulation, planning, implementing decisions, control, communication and so on. In particular a crucial area of responsibility lies in the field of decision-making since the achievement of the objectives of the organisation depends upon successful decisions. With his colleagues the risk manager has therefore to seek the most effective allocation of of the limited resources of the enterprise in the pursuit of the corporate goals.

The decision problems facing the risk manager are different in nature from those facing the general business manager - i.e. pricing strategy, mix of product, input combination etc. - being concerned rather with whether a risk can be avoided or eliminated, whether it should be analysed, how it can be reduced and the appropriate manner of dealing with the costs as they arise.

In general, the decision process can be divided into four stages:

1. The **identification** of the need for a decision. This is a crucial step as identification always precedes effective treatment.

2. The requirement to **identify** or **generate solutions** appropriate to the environment within which the organisation is operating. In addition to the normal constraint of resources other factors may restrict an organisation ability to pursue courses of action proposed as a solution to the original problem.An awareness of the operating environment is therefore important to the formulation of practical solutions; it is equally important as a means of discerning the pressures and forces in the business world which create the risks to which the risk manager is expected to respond.

3. **Estimation of future variables.** The risk manager is constantly seeking to predict and hence either prevent or reduce the occurrence and impact of loss. To accomplish this much reliance is placed on past data accumulated by either the firm or their insurers and from this seeking to identify trends and extrapolate results for the future. This particular task of the risk manager is dealt with in greater length and detail in a later text.

4. **Decide between competing solutions.** Systematic evaluation of the solutions generated in stage two of the process is carried out and the respective projects ranked as far as possible according to a common denominator. Mathematical and statistical techniques are often employed in the search for an optimal solution and will be the subject of fuller investigation at a later stage in Corporate Risk Management.

In order to make reasonable decisions and contribute effectively to the corporate decision-making process the risk manager therefore requires an appreciation of the "environment" within which the firm is operating.

2.0 Key Points

The purpose of this chapter therefore will be:

- to note briefly the constituent parts of the "business environment";
- to provide a model of the factors that give rise to risk;
- to survey the various concepts and definitions of risk;
- to provide an appreciation of the costs imposed by risk;
- to demonstrate the scope of risk management.

3.0 The Business Environment

Environment in this sense is not confined to the constraints of location and climate but extends to the forces within the society, of which the organisation is an integral part, which shape its beliefs, behaviour and business relationships. In practice these forces are usually reflected in the legislative, political and economic institutions of the country in question. For example, it would be expected that the cultural and therefore the trading environment of the the U.K. would be different from that of one of the nations of the Gulf states as a result of differing belief and value systems.

The business environment can be divided into a number of categories, but for our purposes the following broad areas will be adopted:

- economic
- legal
- socio-political

These classifications reflect the external influences of the business environment of most immediate import to the risk manager, because in many cases they will impinge on the day-to-day management of risk.

3.1 Economic Environment

The economic environment is of importance as the constraint of limited resources affects the risk manager in a similar fashion to the line manager. An understanding of the fundamentals governing decisions about the allocation of scarce resources is therefore essential if the risk manager is to be able to see his function in the wider context of the economic survival of the enterprise.

Furthermore, the business firm is part of the national and international economic community. It cannot therefore be isolated from events on these levels. An overview and broad understanding of the issues involved and consequently the implications of decisions taken by others, usually governments, will assist in an appreciation of the constraints placed on the organisation by external economic factors and the risks which such constraints may pose to the organisation.

3.2 Legal Environment

Laws are the embodiment of rules in a framework within which everyone lives. The patterns of behaviour within a society are then regulated by the rules that the community has devised and which its members recognise as binding on themselves. These rules determine such things as what land we may own, what goods we may have, who we may contract with and the appropriate course of action required in the event of the rules being broken. Broadly speaking English law deals with the following:

a) the behaviour of the State(Constitutional law) and the behaviour of the individual (Criminal law) - referred to as Public Law

b) the rights and duties of the individual - Private Law.

Since all societies share this feature, the risk manager has to be alert to the constraint, the protection and the risk that the legal environment imposes.

Because a legal system reflects the rules of conduct of a society it will be subject to amendment, change or extension of its scope. These developments may also be paralleled by changes in the method of institution, enactment and enforcement of the rules. Modern nations are also increasingly influenced by forces external to themselves in the framing and enactment of their laws, the influence of E.C. legislation in the U.K. being a case in point. The risk manager cannot afford to ignore the effect of these national and international developments on the conduct of business.

3.3 Socio-political Environment

The legislative framework is a reflection of the cultural and belief systems of a society. Moreover is does not simply reflect current attitudes and beliefs but is often the repository of the beliefs and values of previous generations of citizens. This is only reasonable as attitudes, beliefs and values are usually partly shaped by history. Therefore to some degree to understand the rationale of a system of laws an appreciation of the forces which have moulded the system is required.

The risk manager however cannot afford to wait for society to respond to changes in patterns of beliefs and patterns of behaviour through future legislation because such changes may threaten the enterprise in the present. A keen interest and appreciation of the forces which shape a society will place the risk manager in an advantageous position when seeking to identify and respond adequately to risk. A knowledge of these factors can then be profitably applied in a variety of situations.

Finally, a knowledge of the constitution and operation of the political institutions in any country together with an awareness of the political climate will enable the risk manager to identify and respond to threats to the organisation more timeously and therefore effectively.

4.0 Risk

Risk is more than a concept it is a reality. Nationally, it imposes costs in terms of material damage, lost markets, loss of profits, additional production costs, loss of wages and employment, environmental pollution, injury, personal suffering and so on, the extent of which is rarely recognised. The Association of British Insurers (ABI) produce figures annually which indicate something of the extent of the economic and social cost of risk. For example:

— estimated fire damage figures for 1987 amounted to £638.3m.

— £297.4m was paid by employers in respect of claims made against them by employees for injuries sustained at work during 1986.

— claims paid in respect of losses from crime amounted to £655.5m during 1987, £290.3m of which was paid under household policies.

— losses from severe weather conditions (see fig 1.1 below). At the time of writing the costs of damage caused by gale force winds and flooding principally in the South and West of England and Wales during January and February 1990 has been estimated as £2,500m.

Major UK weather incidents

The figures are estimates of the cost to UK insurance companies of specific major weather incidents since 1979.

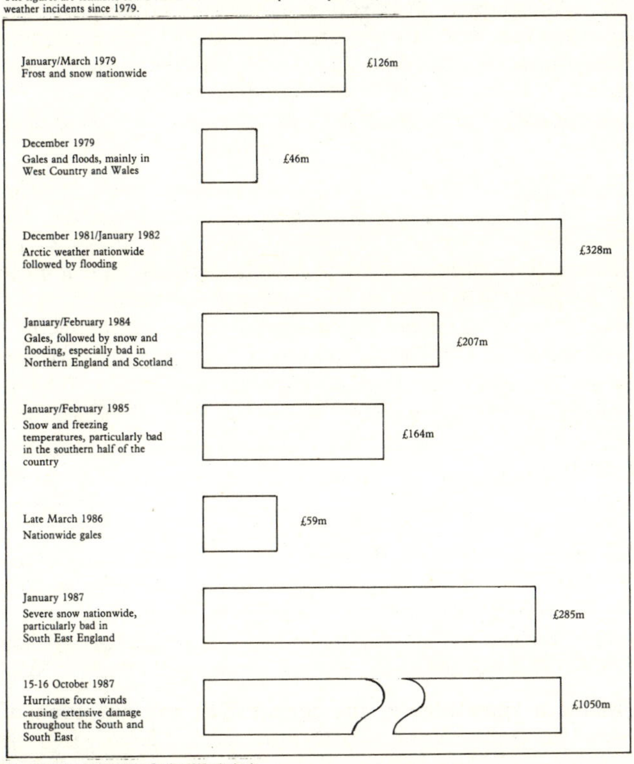

All costs have been re-expressed at October 1987 price levels.

Source: Associated British Insurers
Insurance Statistics 1983-1987

Fig. 1.1

The scale of risk is also perceived to be rising. Peter Drucker writing in the 1950's noted this trend which has accelerated with increased economic and technological sophistication. For example, the costs of decommissioning nuclear power generating stations are proving to be greater than those incurred in their construction. Awareness of the sensitivity of the ecological balance to industrial processes and other examples of humans interaction with their environment has led to the concerns voiced by "green" parties and pressure groups. This has manifested itself to the insurance industry in the growth of environmental liability claims.

Confronted by such potentially catastrophic loss exposures and the continuing drain on resources imposed by less dramatic events, industry and society have reacted through seeking to control and manage the continuing cost of risk. Drucker writing in The Practice of Management (1954) asserted that one of the fundamental requirements of management was that it "should be able to calculate each risk ..., then establish in advance what is expected to happen and to control this subsequent course of action as events bear out or deny these expectations." It is no accident therefore that amongst other initiatives these forces have led to the emergence of a body of knowledge focused on the management of such risks.

According to Bannister and Bawcutt in Practical Risk Management (Witherby 1981), this study was further prompted when business enterprises recognised the increasing amounts of scarce corporate resources being devoted to the financing of risk principally by means of insurance. Figures from a U.S. survey in 1982 indicated that annual aggregate insurance premiums paid by U.S. corporations were on a scale similar to the dividends distributed by these corporations.

Growing interest in the problems of the management of pure risk led to the formation of associations of professionalas concerned with these areas. For example the Association of Insurance and Risk Managers in Industry and Commerce (AIRMIC) in the UK, the Risk and Insurance Management Society, Inc (RIMS) in the U.S. and the Association of Risk and Insurance Managers of Australia (ARIMA). Federations of national bodies such as the Association Europeenne des Assures de l'Industrie (AEAI) which represents member associations at European Community level and the International Federation of Risk and Insurance Management Associations (IFRIMA) have also emerged.

AIRMIC was formed in 1963 to "cater for the special interests of ... insurance managers in ... private and public industry ... commerce and with local authorities" through promotion of greater understanding of the role of risk management, the provision of a forum for the exchange of information and representation of its members views to a wide variety of audiences. These objectives and roles are largely similar to those of its sister organisations. The Association's educational role was formalised in 1986 with the establishment of the Institute of Risk Management (IRM).

Risk management theory and practice has been formulated and has developed as a strategy for dealing with these risks. The fundamental procedures involved in the practice of risk management include:

i) identification of pure risk events that may impose financial losses on the enterprise;

ii) evaluation of the potential costs that would be involved if such events should occur;

iii) estimation of the frequency with which the events might ooccur;

iv) analysis of the alternatives that are available;

v) selection of the most desirable alternative in light of the overall goals of the enterprise at the time the decision is made; and

vi) periodic re-evaluation and monitoring.

The alternative methods of handling those risks that have been identified and measured usually fall into one of the following categories:

a) avoid the activity giving rise to loss;

b) transfer financial responsibility for loss arising from the risk to a third party other than an insurer;

c) reduce the frequency and/or severity of the loss;

d) retain the risk;

e) insure the risk.

Options *c, d* and *e* are not mutually exclusive.

The handling devices *b-e* normally involve two different types of finance functions, namely investment and financing. For example investment decisions are concerned with loss reduction and prevention projects and financing decisions entail the selection of suitable sources of finance for either loss reduction projects or the replacement of destroyed resources (options *b, d, e.*)

The approach represented schematically below in figure 1/2 divides the process into three stages of measurement, control and financing which cover all the procedures described earlier.

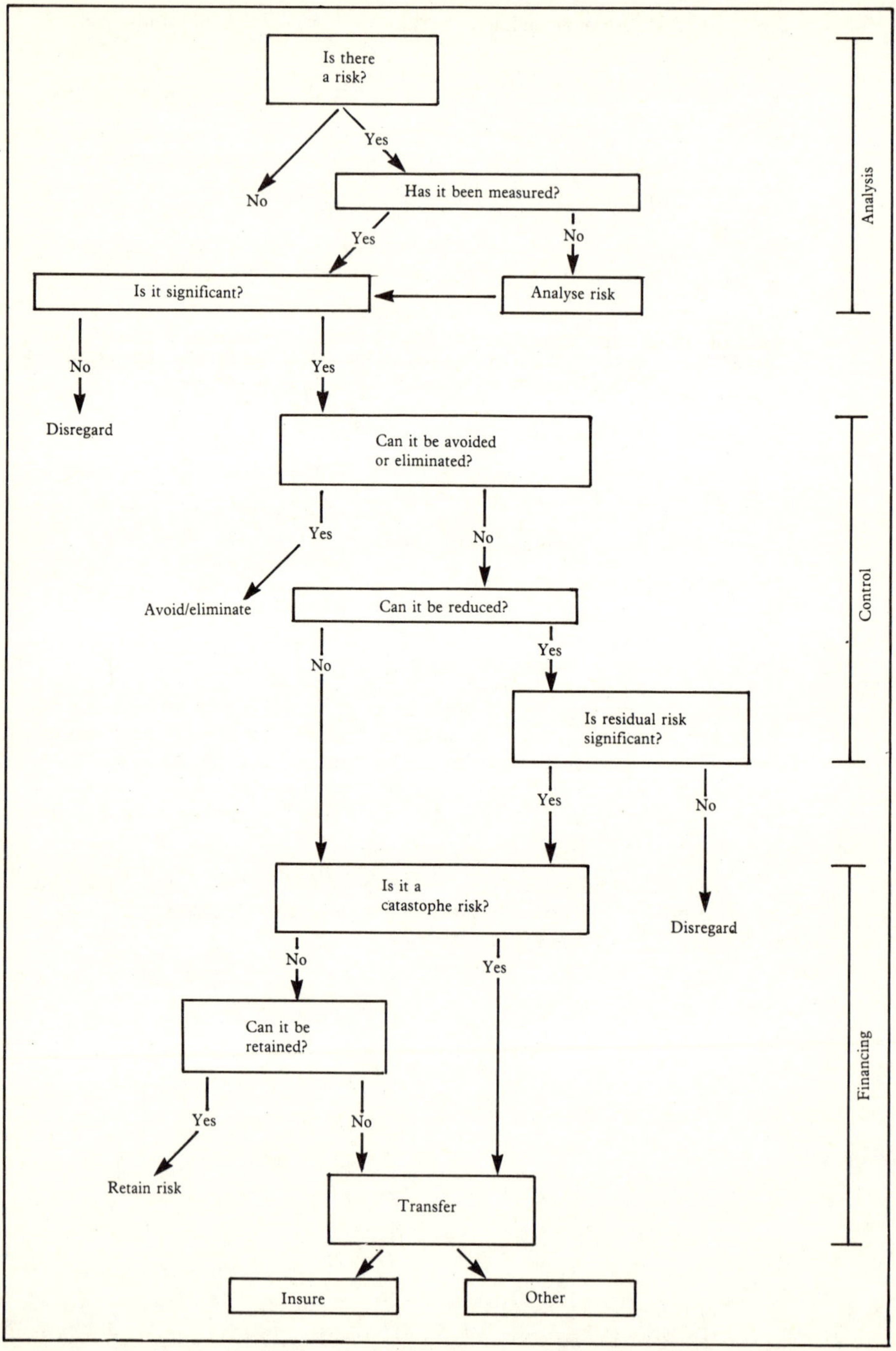
Is there
a risk?
Yes
No
Has it been measured?
Yes
No
Is it significant?
Analyse risk
No
Yes
Disregard
Can it be avoided
or eliminated?
Yes
No
Avoid/eliminate
Can it be reduced?
No
Yes
Is residual risk
significant?
Yes
No
Is it a
catastophe risk?
Disregard
No
Yes
Can it be
retained?
Yes
No
Retain risk
Transfer
Insure
Other
Analysis
Control
Financing

Fig. 1/2

4.1 The Origin of Risk

A fundamental aspect of risk is the uncertainty or doubt attributable to the outcome of a particular action. The nature of a business enterprise infers that an organisation embarks upon decisions unsure of many of the factors which will determine the eventual outcome of the decision. The organisation therefore operates in the area of doubtful knowledge. The areas of uncertainty arise from the relationships which any organisation is obliged to maintain with other groups in society in order to pursue its goals.

Although all parties are mutually dependant on the health of the relationships that exist, this does not imply that these are trouble-free as each of the groups acting out of their interests will tend to place strains on these relationships. Dr Dickson has depicted the situation as represented in Figure 1/3.

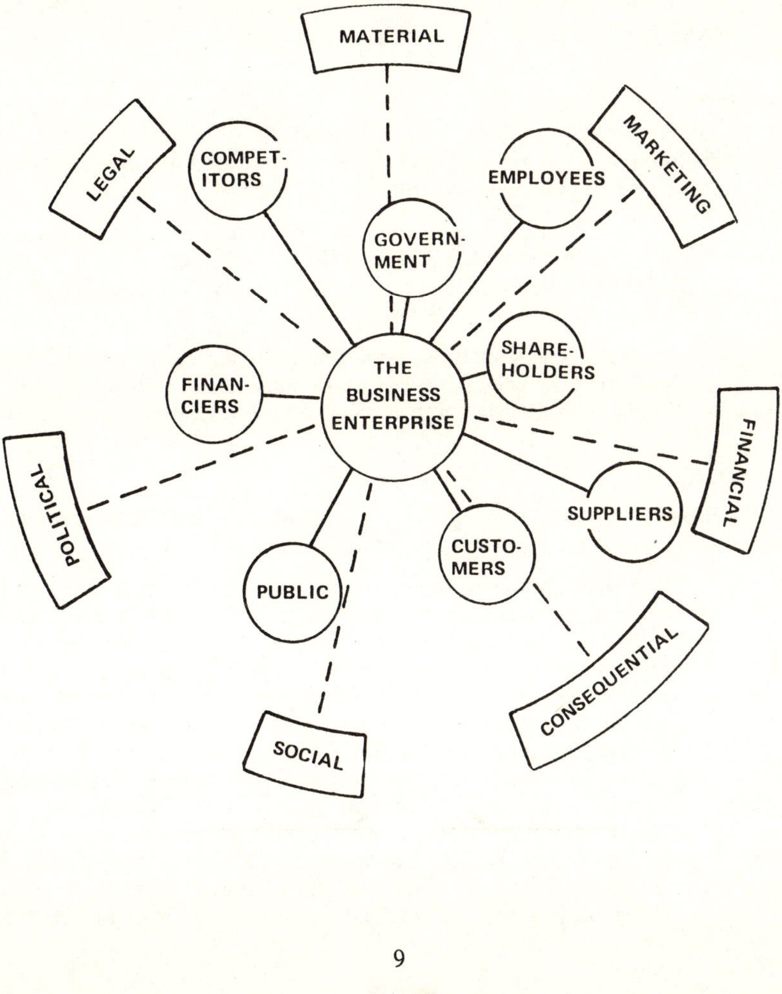

The firm is seen as being at the centre of a number of relationships with different groups in society - or spheres as they are represented in the model. These are variously Government, employees, shareholders, suppliers, customers, financiers, competitors and the public. The spheres are free to move about of their own accord which inevitably produces "collisions". The collisions are simply clashes of interest such as employees against shareholders or employees against Government. They can either affect the firm indirectly, as in the examples cited above, or directly for example in the arena of business/customer relationships. According to Dr Dickson the result of the collisions - the "friction" - is doubt, since the timing, locality, or outcome of the collision is unknown. It matters little whether the collision actually occurs, the mere possibility creates doubt. Risk arises therefore as a result of alteration in the state of nature - in other words, as the result of change.

If the risk manager is to effectively manage the risks to which the firm is subject, he will require at least an appreciation of the forces creating those risks, hence the arguements in favour of risk management as a multi-disciplinary function.

4.2 Risk and Uncertainty

Professor Frank Knight in *Risk, Uncertainty and Profit,* published in 1921 (reprinted by Harper and Row, 1965) identified uncertain events as following into two main categories

– those for which the probability of occurrence can be calculated either on a rational, *a priori,* basis, or on the basis of the statistical analysis of a number of similar events that have occurred in the past. These are risks.

– those for which analysis is impossible by virtue of the fact that they are either a "one-off" event or because their occurrence does not follow an apparent pattern of events. These are uncertainties.

4.3 Definition

Following Professor Knight's classification risk can be measured in a number of ways:

1. **The probability of occurrence,** or the chance that an event may take place. Probability is usually defined as the number of occasions a particular event will occur in an infinitely large number of independent events. It is measured either as a decimal, a fraction or as a percentage but always in the range 0 to 1. In other words probabilities range from there being no chance that the event will occur to the certainty that it will occur. Note that certainty is here defined as a 100% probability of occurrence. Examples include the probability of an unbiased coin landing on its head or tail, or the likelihood of drawing the Ace of Spades from an unmarked, full and fair pack of cards. The examples cited above can be calculated on an *a priori* basis but others like the chance of damage to property or person can only be resolved by recourse to statistical evidence.

Probability is however an average concept - that is, it depends on the occurrence of a large number of events. Consider the coin-tossing example cited above. It is unlikely that if the operation were performed 10 time that the ratio of heads to tails would be exactly 1:1, yet logically (discounting the possibility that the coin would come to rest on its side) this should be the case. This is borne out but only after a large number of experiments; the larger the number of experiments the closer the actual result approaches the expected result. This is in fact the operation of the law of large numbers: as the number of events increases, the relative variation in actual from expected outcome decreases. From the practical point of view therefore the probability of occurrence is of restricted value as its accuracy depends on the number of items at risk. For example if a firm has 10 vehicles which have a 10% or 1 in 10 chance of being involved in accident it knows that, on average, one vehicle per year will incur accidental damage. There is however no certainty that another one or more vehicles will not be damaged. On the other hand, a large haulage firm with 5000 vehicles with a similar incidence rate can reasonably confidently predict that the number of vehicles damaged will be 500 per year.

There are a few other problems. Probability is not a certain measurement. A certain measurement of risk requires a complete set of information, but since the complete set of data comprises an infinite amount the probabilities can never be certain. An associated difficulty is that much data is incomplete and often inadequate. The provision of underlying probability from such a base is therefore fraught with difficulty and usually subject to subjective influences.

2. **Deviation in actual from expected outcomes.** In this case risk is a measurement of the degree of variation between expected and actual outcomes. Therefore the greater the variance from the expected outcome the greater the risk. We can consider the above example of motor fleet problems to illustrate this concept.

When a statistical analysis of the occurrence of events is carried out a probability distribution is created. In the example Figure 1/4(a) illustrated below it shows the probabilities of differing numbers of accidents occurring. The probability of no accidents is almost zero, the probability that all vehicles will be involved in some way or other is remote, and between these extremes are ranged all the other possibilities. From this distribution it can be observed that most of the occurrences occur within a relatively narrow range. The risk manager can therefore be fairly confident about his predictions concerning the number of events. The risk is low. Compare this to the picture in Figure 1/4(b) which shows a "flatter" distribution The reasons for this flatness could be many, including lack of data and only a small number of units exposed to the risk. The risk in this case is greater because the measure of variation would be greater in this case than in the former example.

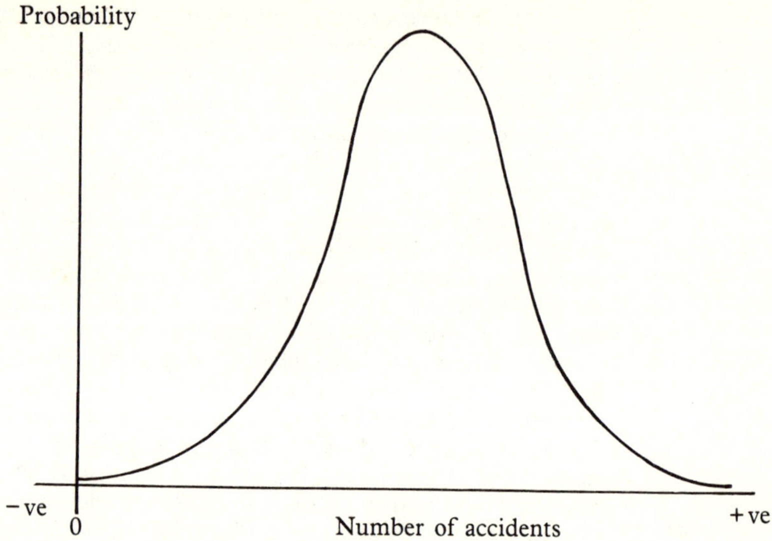

Fig. 1/4(a)

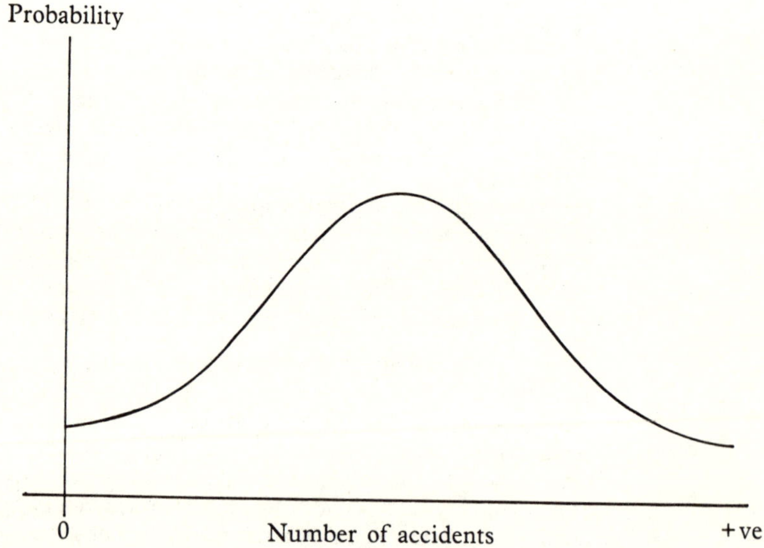

Fig. 1/4(b)

Two main problems emerge with this definition

i) it is based on probabilities which as was discussed above is a far from certain measurement itself. There is, according to Dr Dickson in Decision Theory in Risk Management, the danger of compounding the original error and in fact producing greater inaccuracy.

ii) a lower degree of risk could actually mean that there was a greater chance of loss for the the variance does not take account of whether the values are positive or negative. This problem is illustrated in Figure 1/5 below.

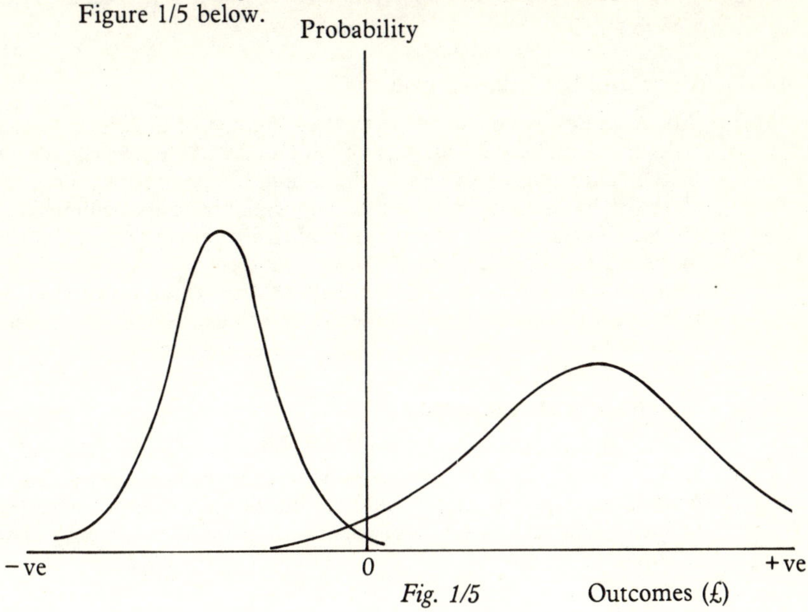

Fig. 1/5

3. **"Downside risk".** This concept discussed by Professor Carter in *Management II: Risk Management* (CII Tuition Service) defines risk as the probability that the outcome of an event falls below some acceptable minimum standard. Combining this with the one discussed above would circumvent the problem that was identified there. Downside risk however depends upon the acceptable level of risk that an organisation would wish to bear, an amount which in itself is subject to variation and is determined by both time-scale and the financial resources of the organisation.

4. **Subjective risk.** From the above discussion a number of theoretical and practical problems have emerged in the measurement of risk. As a result of these difficulties decision-makers often find that they have to make the best with what data is available rely on their own experience and produce subjective estimates of probability. This will always be the result when statistical data is supplemented by individual judgement. Since subjective risk is "the uncertainty of an event as seen or perceived by an individual" (Greene and Serbein in *Risk Management: text and cases)* the estimate of the extent of risk is dependent upon the attitudes of the individual manager which of course can be expected to vary from person to person. Thus a persons attitude to risk will influence the perception and therefore their treatment of the risk. Decisions upon which risks are acceptable or unacceptable to bear may well rest on the risk attitude of the manager concerned.

4.4 Categories of Risk

A number of different terms have been devised to categorise risks according to either the cause, the outcome or the method of tackling the risk concerned.

4.4.1 Pure and speculative risk.

This category is concerned with the outcome of uncertain events. Pure risks are events the occurrence of which result in either the maintenance of the status quo or in loss to the individual or organisation concerned. Pure risk holds out no prospect of gain which is what distinguishes it from speculative risk, where the prospect of either gain or loss exists. Examples of pure risks include fire, theft, fraud and injury, from which it can be seen that in most cases it is unlikely that anything other than loss will result. Entrepreneurial risk undertaken by businessmen is an example of speculative risk where either profit or loss may result.

4.4.2 Dynamic and static risks

These are more properly identified with the factors causing change. Dynamic risks are those associated with changes in society and arise from market, management and/or political forces and can result in either profit or loss. Static risks are independent of these movements and result only in loss.

4.4.3 Fundamental and particular risks

Fundamental risks are those which affect if not the whole of society at least a large proportion of it and arise from natural disasters or changes in the political or economic system. They are impersonal in the sense that they are not caused by the individual and they affect society as a whole. Particular risks are to some degree under the control of the individual or organisation concerned and affect only the party incurring the risk. A somewhat imperfect example may be if an individual chooses to leave his employment during a period of full employment and fails to secure another position immediately, the resulting unemployment could br the particular risk that the individual undertook when resigning in the first place. If however unemployment was a feature of the economic environment this would be regarded as a fundamental risk.

4.4.4 "Commercial" and "insurable" risk

These terms are used by Bannister and Bawcutt in *Practical Risk Management* to denote the division in treatment that risk has received from academics. The principal distinction, which we discussed above, is that while some risks are amenable to insurance - e.g. static and pure risks - others are not. These commercial risks are normally associated with speculative or dynamic risks and are usually regarded as being uninsurable. The inference is then that only insurable risks should be the proper concern of the risk manager. Bannister & Bawcutt reject this division.

This position is made on the grounds of the "trade-off" which they contend takes place when an insurance premium is paid. The trade-off in this case is between the payment of the premium and the assurance that funds will be forthcoming in the event of a loss which is akin to the trade-off that occurs when a capital expenditure is made in the present against the expectation of higher returns over the medium to longer term. The trade-off being the commitment of funds now in the expectation of higher returns in the future.

Their argument is supported by an appeal to utility theory. In utility theory, a purchase will be made if the purchaser perceives that it will produce additional personal benefit. Thus all purchases involve an element of trade-off between the loss of utility of the cash paid and the utility gained by the purchase. Bannister and Bawcutt argue that since all sales/purchases include the twin benefits of reduction of risk and provision of service this analysis can be easily applied to the purchase of insurance. The price depends on the proportions in which each element is present and the preferences of the individual. This analysis can also be applied to the sale of any goods supporting their contention that insurable risks and commercial risks are merely opposite ends of the same spectrum.

Furthermore the belief that insurable risk is concerned with a loss only situation is challenged by appeal to the existence of the "moral hazard" problem as evidence that insurable risk may also produce the possibility of gain. Finally, the reader is referred to the societal benefits of insurance as an answer to the point that most insurance is viewed by the purchaser as an unpleasant decision and that many insurances are compulsory.

The conclusion is that many of the techniques that have been developed for dealing with insurable risks could be applied with equal profit to commercial risks and that the risk manager's activities and remit should not be circumscribed by this false division.

4.5 Types of Risk

The classification adopted by Bannister and Bawcutt reflect the points discussed above and encompasses both "commercial" and "insurable" risks. Thus the risks faced by the business enterprise fall into three main categories:

i) those which potentially are at least partially manageable by management such as physical damage, liability etc

ii) those directly controllable by management including risks normally associated with commercial management such as staff selection and control

iii) those which are not under the direct control of management but which may be manageable to some degree or other such as the social, political and physical environment. These risks however include circumstances from which loss or gain may result.

In terms of the Figure 1/3 the risk manager is concerned with those areas of doubt identified as:

MATERIAL	–	fire, corrosion, explosion, fraud, structural defect, war.
CONSEQUENTIAL	–	loss of profit following fire, theft, pollution, strikes
SOCIAL	–	moral liability, consumer pressure
LEGAL	–	statutory liability, contract conditions
POLITICAL	–	governmental intervention, sanctions, acts of foreign governments.

The first risk that can arise is physical loss or damage to property and injury or death to people. These may be caused by changes in the natural environment - flood, fire etc - but may in fact be the result of malicious acts. A second is the risk of liability arising from claims made against the organisation by its employees or the general public. A third is the loss to earnings caused by an interruption to production by the occurrence of one the events listed, or alternatively, caused by poor publicity following an award of damages to a customer for injuries etc that arose from the consumption of one of the products of the company. A further loss that can arise is through errors in management. Poor staff selection may lead to poor resource allocation decisions or industrial relation problems; or poor control in other areas may allow problems for which there are solutions if actioned timeously, but which may become uncontrollable if ignored. The losses that arise through wastage are further examples of events within the control of management. Inadequate stock control, lack of proper maintenance and poor design usually give rise to small-scale losses but may in some circumstances be responsible for a large-scale loss.

Companies are also subject to changes in social, political and economic factors. Social change is a major factor in risk. Social attitudes to work, the role of government, the equitable distribution of income, the authorities etc affect the risk profile of the organisation. The means by which information is disseminated and opinion influenced is another important factor which has been particularly prominent over the past 30 years with growth of the acceptance of means of mass communication. Social change has proceeded at at pace hitherto unknown in social history. Companies and individuals alike are vulnerable to political risk. Both have to bear the consequence of inflationary or deflationary economic policies adopted by successive governments or be subject restrictions on the export or import of capital or goods. Also, the increasing volume of legislation enacted in democratic societies imposes additional constraints and costs and reduces the ability to compete. Further uncertainty is built in to the system as a result of periodic change of government and economic policies. Economically, changes in the methods of production and distribution are another source of risk. Modern economies are highly interdependent, and changes in technology usually lead to an increase in this as well as an increase in both the values at risk and the extent potential damage. The environmental impact of the malfunction of a nuclear reactor is likely to be greater than that of its coal or oil-fired counterparts. Equally, decisions about stock control, means of distribution and the management of cash flow involve risk which may lead to loss. For example, if a firm decides to operate a credit policy towards potential customers it opens itself to the possibility that some of its debtors may eventually be unwilling or unable to pay.

Whilst some of these risks have traditionally been regarded as insurable, there are others which have not but yet would represent a threat to the firm. It should be recognised therefore that insurable risk is only a sub-set of the risks with which the risk manager should expect to concern himself.

4.6 The Cost of Risk.

The costs imposed by the existence of risk can be identified in three separate areas:

i) **the cost of the loss.** This includes both direct and indirect costs. Direct costs being those immediately attributable the event - e.g. repairs to a damaged vehicle, replacement of goods damaged as the result of a collision, third party compensation if necessary, assessor's expenses etc. Indirect costs in this example may be additional wear and tear on other vehicles and time lost by other drivers attending the scene of the accident.

ii) **costs of handling risk.** Time spent on identification, analysis and negotiation of insurance covers could be more profitably employed in income-generating activities. The additional monetary costs of loss prevention and reduction together with the costs of consultancy fees and insurers' profit loading serve to reduce the profitability of the company.

iii) **costs imposed by risk.** Because we live in an uncertain world, individuals are willing to pay amounts in excess of the sums which they stand to lose, on average, in the long term i.e. over their lifetime. This is known as the expected value of loss, the calculation of which is as follows:

Example:

Imagine you own an antique valued at £250,000. To most of us this would be a fortune and therefore we would be anxious to ensure it remained in good condition and under our control. The fact that you are uncertain about its fate from one year to the next indicates that you are subject to uncertainty. The value of the antique is no longer £250,000 because that was its value under conditions of certainty. Its value under uncertainty can be calculated by reference to measures of uncertainty derived from statistics. The probability of theft or destruction can be calculated by reference to past statistics because these are repeatable events. The expected loss can then be calculated as

$$\text{Total wealth before loss} \times \text{probability of occurrence}$$
$$+ \text{ Wealth after loss} \times (1 - \text{probability of occurrence})$$
$$= \text{Expected value of loss}$$

Thus the expected value of loss in the above example where there

$$£250{,}000(0.1) + £0(1 - 0.1)$$
$$= £25{,}000$$

This the statistical value of a 10% risk of loss. It is often referred to as the **pure loss.**

This however is not the final cost. The owner of the valuable antique will most probably be prepared to pay more than the pure loss to an insurer to be covered against the financial effect of any loss. The amount in excess of the pure loss paid in the form of premium to the insurer is the measure of the cost of risk that individual.

Another implication of risk averse behaviour is the fear of failure. Since there is a greater desire to avoid loss then certain projects which may be beneficial to the community at large may be unacceptable to the producer because of the risk of severe loss. The producer may require higher rewards than is statistically warranted with the result that the risk is avoided and production does not take place.

Together these represent the total direct and indirect costs of risk. It is not possible to quantify all of them nor to predict who will bear them.

Conventionally private costs refer to the individual or business incurring them in the course of pursuing the activity creating the risk. It is often difficult however to confine those costs to their creator. Social costs of risk fall upon the community at large. The risks associated with the storage of dangerous chemicals in an urban community are not borne solely by the firm concerned, as becomes evident in the event of leakage or explosion.

Thus increasing social awareness has brought about a realization of the costs imposed on society and calls for the creators of those risks to redress the balance in some way either by adopting more stringent safety standards or working practices or by compensation payments to affected parties, even where there may not be a legal obligation to do so.

4.0 Summary and Conclusion

This chapter has been concerned with establishing the nature and scope of risk management. In doing so we have considered the similarity of the role of the the risk managers to other managers in the business enterprise as well as the distinctive contribution that it can make to the organisation. We then considered a diagrammatic representation of the factors leading to existence of risk for an individual organisation and noted the chief sources of those risks together with a classification of the range of outcomes that would arise from the occurrence of the events identified.

We discovered that "risk" is not a homogeneous concept. It can be measured as either the probability of occurrence or as the variability in outcomes. Furthermore it can be classified according the cause or the outcome of the risk and as argued by Bannister and Bawcutt should not be divided too quickly into whether it is commercial or insurable risk.

Finally we noted the costs that arose as the consequence of the existence of risk, classifying them as the costs of loss, the costs of handling risk and the costs imposed by the existence of risk.

Chapter Two

THE ECONOMIC ENVIRONMENT — Supply and Demand

1.0 Introduction

The basic problem for mankind is the provision of those goods and services that make life possible — namely, food, clothing and shelter — needs which are basic to all the peoples of the world. And the needs are great, with the current world population of approximately 3 billion and forecasted to be at least 6 billion by AD 2000.

In order to meet this demand production has to be organised, either by individuals or groups. Since goods and services can be produced for consumption by other than those involved in their production then distribution has to be organised to deliver these supplies to those with the demand. In this event arrangements have to be made that are acceptable to producers and consumers for the valuation and payment of goods provided.

And of course once the goods or services have been consumed the whole process begins anew. In some cases this may be measured in days whilst others may be measured in years, but it is a continuous cycle of production and consumption.

Economics is concerned with these daily issues of the organisation of production, its distribution and the means of payment. As Alfred Marshall, an eminent Victorian economist said economics is 'the study of mankind in everyday life'. The issue however is more than simply one of organisation.

There is another factor to consider, namely the problem of unlimited human wants and finite resources which is the fundamental economic problem.

The upshot of this dilemma is that all societies have had to devise a system of prioritising these wants and allocating the scarce resources accordingly. The problem is illustrated graphically below:

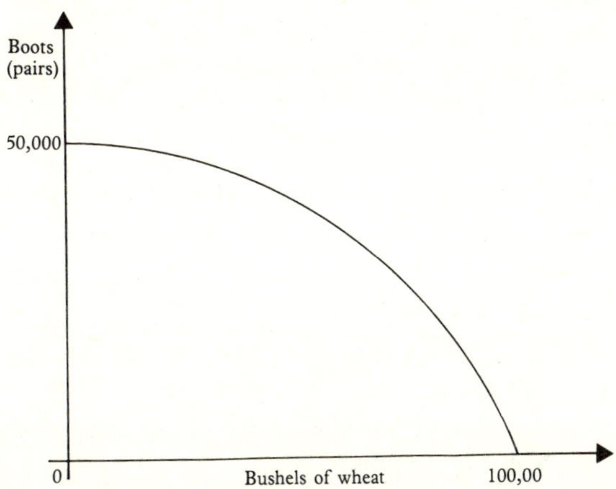

Fig. 2/1

This is a production possibilities curve and depicts the choices open to the citizens of Fridonia, a state with a simple economic system. Utlilising all the resources available, production of wheat amounts to 100,000 bushels per annum. On the other hand, if resources are concentrated in the manufacture of rubber boots 50,000 pairs can be produced in the same time. This represents the total production of the country, and the curve represents all possible of combination of production of these items. Note however that each additional pair of boots produced is only accomplished by sacrificing a certain number of bushels of wheat. (Any combination lying below the curve would indicate unemployed resources.) The choices facing the people of Fridonia, as in all other societies are those of what should be produced, in what numbers, in what manner and how should the goods (or wealth) then be distributed amongst the citizens of the country. Different societies throughout history have adopted varying approaches to these problems. These have included allocation on the basis of tradition, or prices or by a central body or person. The centrally planned economy is a feature of communist societies and some less developed nations. The **price** or **market** system emphasises the role of "market forces" in the derivation of price and subsequently the part played by prices in the allocation decision. This is a feature of many "Western" economies.

Those societies which have adopted the market system to a greater or lesser extent are however not wholly dependant on it. For a number of reasons these societies have deemed it acceptable that the allocation of a proportion their resources be by non-market mechanisms. Thus the state as a resource-allocator in the economic system and the ensuing development of the mixed economy.

An economic system can be viewed from either the perspective of the individual economic unit - be it either household, firm or industry - or from the the perspective of the system as a whole. The first approach is usually referred to in economic texts as the **micro-economic** view, the latter being known as the **macro-economic** approach. This chapter will be concerned with a brief description of the organisation of production within a mixed economy and an examination of the forces at work in a market economy, followed by a chapter examining production from a microeconomic viewpoint. Chapter 4 will be devoted to a macroeconomic analysis of economic activity and the consequential implications for economic policy. The closing chapter of the section will consider the impact, importance and implications of international trade.

2.0 Key Points

The purpose of this chapter is:

- to examine the interrelationships and note the interdependencies that exist in the modern economy;
- to note the respective roles of the private and public sectors in the modern mixed economy;
- analyse the determination of price in the market;

- provide a framework from which predictions about the result of changes in the market can be made;
- note the extent of consumers reaction to changes in price, and the factors determining the magnitude of this change; and
- examine the insurance purchasing decision with the aid of utility theory.

3.0 The Cycle of Production

The **cycle of production,** figure 2/2 opposite, illustrates the system of allocation and distribution of resources that society has developed in response to the requirement to fulfill the "wants" of its members.

The cycle also illustrates the fact that all economies can be divided according to those responsible for production and those who consume this output. It should not be difficult to see that the persons involved in both activities are in fact one and the same but performing different functions. The owners of land, labour and capital offer their services in return for payment from the producers. The goods which are produced and then sold provide the revenue for producers from which factors are then paid. The income received by the factors is then used to purchase the goods and services necessary to satisfy their respective wants. And so the process continues.

The result is that there are two flows which take place between producers and households within an economy:

i) real flows of goods, services and the services of factors; and

ii) money flows of revenue, wages, interest etc.

The Economic System

Within a market economy, resource allocation decisions about what should be produced how much, the methods of production and how the products should be allocated between the members of society are determined by the forces of supply and demanded. These forces can be seen operating between producers (or suppliers) and consumers in the product markets for manufactured goods and services. They also operate in the factor markets where producers bargain with the factors of production for their services in order to produce goods for sale to consumers.

3.1 The Factors of Production

The scarce resources referred to in the previous section are referred to collectively as the **factors of production** and individually are known as:

LAND – which refers to the natural resources with which a nation has been endowed. It includes mineral and agricultural resources and extends beyond the land mass into coastal waters in certain cases - notably the U.K. Thus crops, animal herds, oil, coal, gas, fish are part of "land".

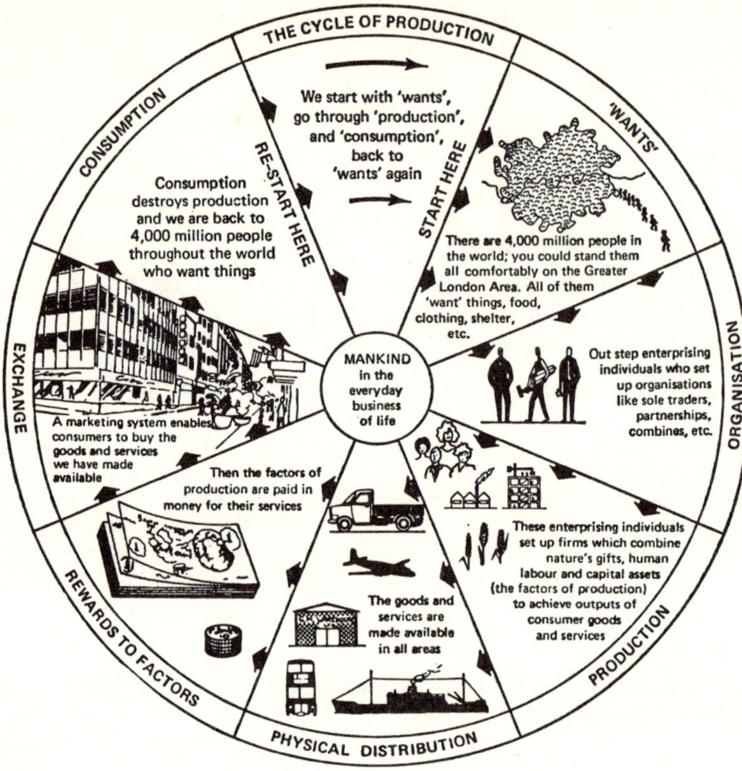

Fig. 2/2

All factors of production have to be rewarded for the provision of their services for a particular use - otherwise they will "offer" their services to another buyer who will be prepared to pay. The reward paid to land is known as **rent.** It usually is based not on the value of the land *per se* but the use to which it can be put. Hence the difference in land "values" between the City of London and the North-West of England.

LABOUR – the human resources of a nation. It is usually measured by the size of the working population. It refers to all aspects of human activity from ingathering and refining of natural resources through the creation of the manufacturing process, the distribution and marketing of the products and the provision of financial, management, professional and medical services.

The reward paid to labour for its services is referred to as **wages.** Within the mixed economy the determination of the level of reward is the product of a number factors such as the demand for the services or skill of the particular of labour and institutional arrangements such as the the degree of organisation amongst those offering themselves for work i.e. the extent of e.g. trades union involvement.

CAPITAL – the resources which have been created by the diversion of economic activity from the production of goods for current consumption - e.g. machine tools and other equipment. The creation of capital goods always infers a cost in terms of foregone consumption, but must be sustained in order to replace obsolete and worn-out equipment and create new more efficient methods of production if a nation is to prosper economically. Note that the term capital always refers to these goods and never to money. It also allows a distinction to be drawn between producer or capital goods and consumer goods which are produced - using capital goods - for immediate consumption.

The reward paid to capital is known as **interest** and is said to be the reward for consumption foregone.

ENTREPRENEUR – this term is employed to indicate the person(s) responsible for the organisation of the the other factors of production. The entrepreneur therefore became the bearer of risk as the organisation of the means of production was financed from his own resources. This still applies to many small businesses where ownership is concentrated in one or two persons, but within the modern business organisation is often linked to the ability to identify or create a market and exploit its potential. Risk however is still borne by the organisation as these operations will be financed from within its own resources.

As with the other factors, the entrepreneur will not operate without reward, this being called **profit.** Without the reward of a satisfactory level of profit the entrepreneur will not be prepared to bear the risk involved. This is an important point as profit in economic terms is a cost of production and not the excess of revenue over "costs" as is the case for the accountant.

3.2 The Mixed Economy

We have noted that the principal groups in an economy are those of households and producers. This however does not reflect the position in a modern economy since in the modern economy an important part of the cycle of production is the active role played by the state. It is no longer confined to the sidelines or to the role of referee, but now has a significant part in the economic life of most developed societies. Thus in many instances it may be the single largest purchaser or supplier. The **mixed economy** therefore is characterised by the economic activity of both the *public* - that is owned by government - and *private* - i.e. owned by private individuals or groups of individuals - sectors.

4.0 The Business Environment

The business environment is influenced and affected by the role played by government in the economic, legal and institutional spheres of the life of the country. Given these conditions firms will seek to survive and prosper through seeking to satisfy the "wants" of consumers in competition with other producers. The business environment is therefore a blend of a number of different activities directed towards the objectives of survival and growth and involves the firm in forecasting demand, planning investment, competing under differing market conditions, raising finance and negotiating with suppliers, consumers and organised labour.

Fundamental to the allocation of a nation's resources within a market economy is the efficient operation of the price mechanism. This is necessary for the allocation of the necessary resources from the factor markets in order to meet the demand of consumers. Therefore the operation of the price mechanism is driven by the forces of demand and supply, irrespective of the market concerned. It should be noted however that the terminology of supply and demand is most frequently associated with analyses of the product markets.

5.0 The Price Mechanism

Price is determined by the interplay of the forces of supply - the producers, and demand - the consumers. The term "supplier" can refer to a wide range of individuals and businesses from manufacturers of electrical goods for households to persons offering their labour for hire. Similarly "consumer" can refer to households or multi-national corporations.

5.1 Demand

Economists employ the term **effective demand** to distinguish between the amount purchased by consumers within a given time period at a specific price from the general wants and desires of consumers. It is this concept of demand that will be referred throughout the remainder of the text.

5.1.2 Demand curves

The relationship between the price of a good and the quantity demanded is known as the **Law of Demand,** which states:

> "the higher the price the lower is the quantity demanded per unit of time".

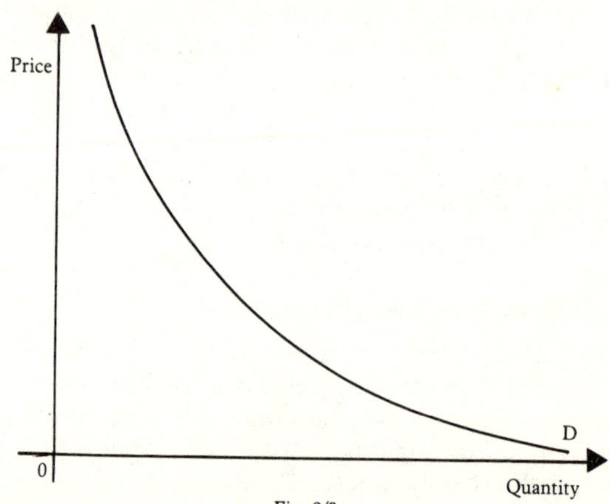

Fig. 2/3

This relationship can be depicted in the form of a demand schedule or more conveniently the demand curve, as in figure 2/3, the main feature of which is that it slopes downward from left to right, displaying the inverse relationship between price and demand.

5.1.3 Conditions of demand

These are the factors that determine what the demand for a particular product will be. They are:

- the **price** of the good in question;
- the **price of other goods;**
- the **income** of buyers;
- the **tastes and preferences** of buyers;
- the **number of buyers,** which is dependant on the size and age distribution of the populations of the countries in which the supplier is operating.

The demand within any particular country will also be affected by factors specific to the country concerned, such as:

- the **level of economic activity,** because consumers in employment have more to spend;
- the **distribution of income,** because demand in a society with a less unequal distribution of rewards will be higher. Societies with highly unequal distributions have lower demand because a) lower paid can afford only basic commodities and live at or below subsistence levels; b) the small minority in receipt of a large proportion of the nation's income spend only a small fraction of additional income received.
- **availability of finance** etc. allows purchasing to be spread over time thus spreading the cost.

Changes in each of these conditions can affect the demand curve as illustrated in figures 2/4a and 2/4b.

> A change in the price of the commodity in question will produce a **movement along the curve** resulting in a contraction or expansion in demand. In figure 2/4a this is the movement from OP_1 to OP_2 giving rise to the change in demand of OQ_1 to OQ_2;
>
> Changes in one of the other factors will result in a **wholesale shift** of the demand curve, giving rise to an increase in demand - OQ_1 to OQ_2 in figure 2/4b - without necessarily being accompanied by an increase in price.

One way of thinking about the difference between the two is that a shift in the curve will mean that demand can expand/contract without a change in price, whereas in the other instance the change in demand is the result of a change in the price in the good.

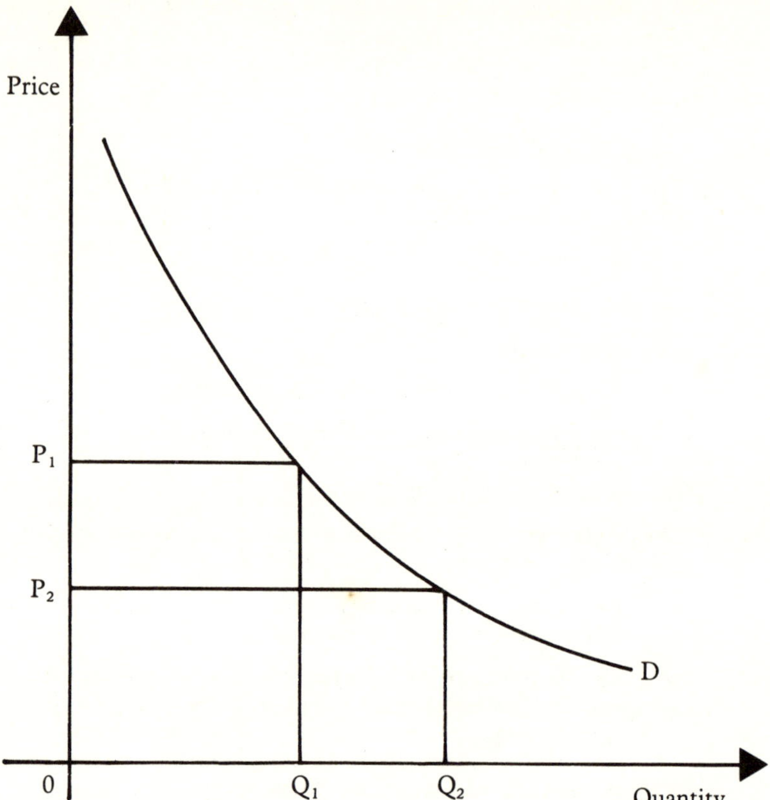

Fig. 2/4a

The **Law of Demand** is described as a "law", because it holds good in most cases. Even where it does not seem to operate - for example, regressive demand curves - these cases can be explained as *exceptions* to the rule because of particular circumstances. The effects of the reaction of consumers to changes in price can be explained in terms of the **income and substitution effects** of a change in price.

The **substitution effect** arises when a customer faced with a rise in the price of goods switches consumption to a competing good which is relatively less expensive.

The **income effect** arises as the result of an increase in price without a similar rise in income thus effectively reducing income. Expenditure on all will therefore have to be be curtailed if consumption of the good undergoing the rise in price is to be maintained.

The reaction of a consumer to any changes in price will depend on the relative strengths of the income and substitution effects. When the price

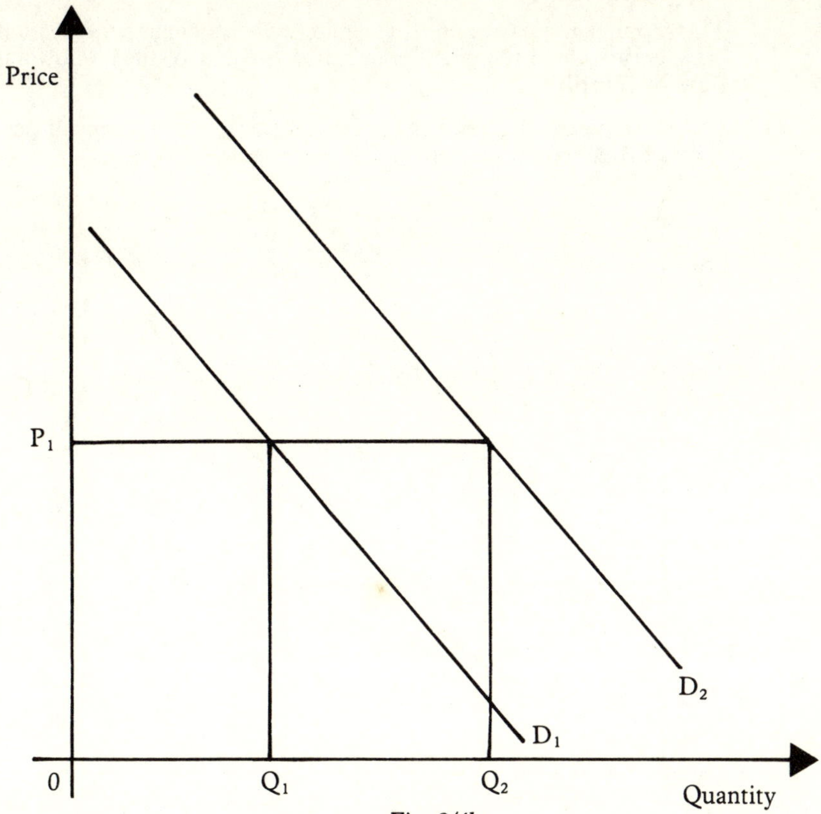

Fig. 2/4b

of a good rises, all others remaining constant, income is effectively reduced and so also will be consumption. In addition other goods will now be relatively cheaper with the effect that consumption will now be switched away from the relatively dearer good.

Exceptions to the law of demand can be explained by reference to these effects and include those goods identified as "goods of ostentation", "inferior" goods and "Giffen" goods. In addition the behaviour "middlemen" may also lead to a reversal of the price-quantity relationship.

5.2 Supply

The production which takes place to meet demand is motivated by the desire for profit on the part of of the producers.

Supply is usually defined as:

> "the quantity of a good or service made available to consumers at a given price in a given period of time".

5.2.1 Supply curve

The supply curve, as depicted in figure 2/5, also depicts the relationship between price and the quantity supplied per unit of time, known as the **Law of Supply:**

> "the higher the price the greater is the quantity supplied per unit of time".

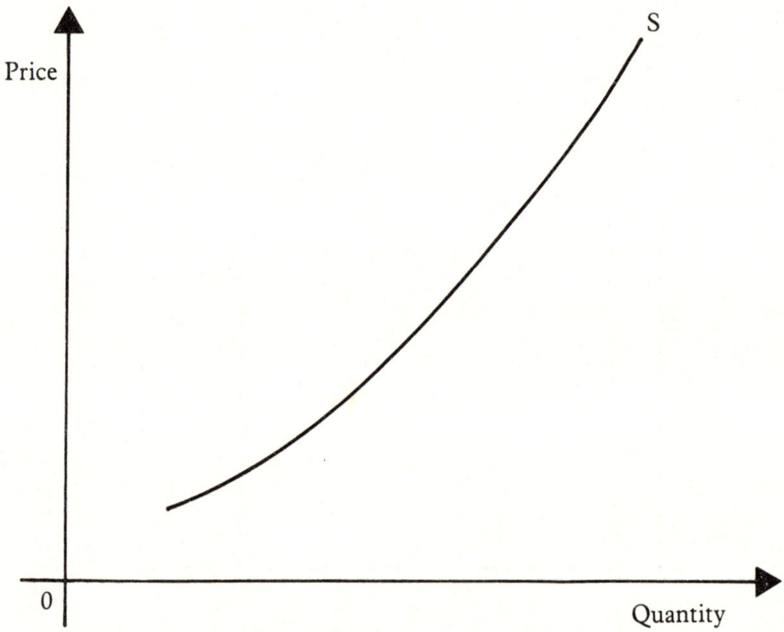

Fig. 2/5

Note that, in contrast to demand, the relationship between price and quantity supplied is a direct one.

5.2.2 Conditions of supply

The factors which influence producers decision to supply are:

- change in the **price** of the good being produced. Since producers are motivated by profit, they will seek to produce the maximum of the most profitable goods, under given cost conditions.
- changes in the **prices of other goods.** If the prices of other goods increase as a result of increased demand, production will be switched towards these because of the increased profit potential.
- changes in the **prices of the factors of production.** These include the prices paid for raw materials, fuel and power, interest charges, rents and wages. Movements in factor prices affect the costs of production and can increase/reduce profits accordingly. Rises in

factor costs may be offset by increased productivity; if they are not, the supply curve will move to the left.

- **climatic conditions and location.** Agricultural products are the most obvious casualties of such factors. Increased costs as the result of unfavourable conditions are however passed on to the rest of the economy. An unfavourable location may impose additional building, safety or transport costs.
- **technology.** This refers to the manner in which a good is produced. Improvements in technology can refer to improvements in the performance of machines and labour, in the quality of raw materials, in organisation and management, in factory layouts, in communications, in techniques of production etc. These usually constitute the main sources of improvements in productivity and will increase supply if costs remain unchanged.
- **taxation and subsidies.** An indirect tax in effect represents an increase in the cost of production of the commodity with the concomitant result for supply. A subsidy reduces the cost of production.

5.3 Determination of Price

In the market economy the reconciliation of the contending forces of supply and demand occurs in the market place. The result is an equilibrium price which "clears" the market which is determined by the

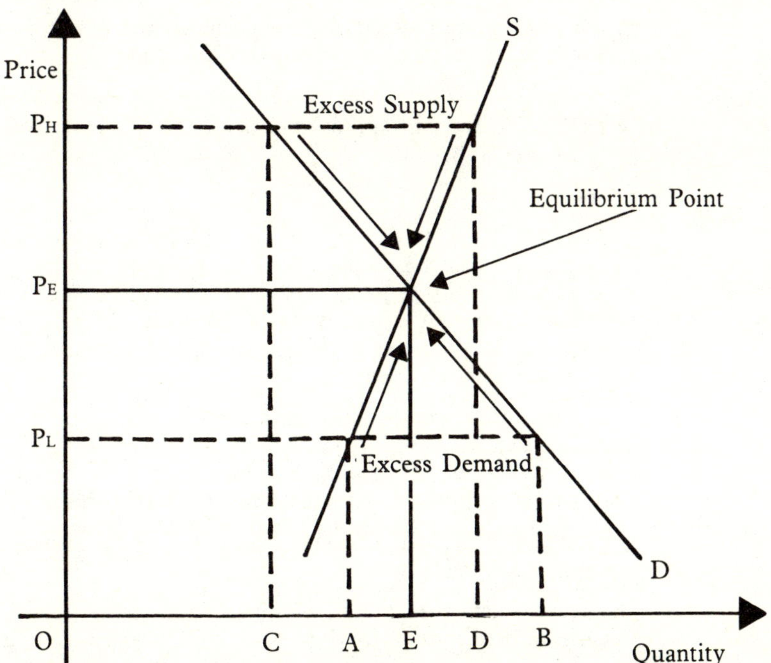

Fig. 2/6

process of the forces of **excess demand** and **excess supply** in the market. Lower than equilibrium prices will create excess demand whilst higher than equilibrium prices will create excess supply. The operation of these opposing forces will push the market towards the equilibrium point at OP_E as illustrated in figure 2/6.

If prices in the market are set at OP_L then demand exceeds supply by AB. Excess demand will drive prices up as producers realise that higher prices can be charged as some consumers are willing to meet these costs.

If prices in the market are OP_H, supply exceeds demand by CD. Producers are therefore forced to cut prices in order to clear backlogs of unsold goods.

The ensuing result of suppliers allocating resources to products which will sell in the market and only in sufficient quantity to meet demand is the argument in favour of the price mechanism as an efficient allocator of resources. In a mixed economy however this is not the only mechanism. Allocation and production decisions are based solely on the economic basis of "demand", and exclude other considerations that society may wish to be taken into account eg social, environmental and moral issues. This infers that society or the state may wish from time to time to interfere with the market mechanism. The results of this intervention can be analysed with the tools developed above.

5.3.1 Application

Using the price/quantity relationships encapsulated in the curves, it is possible to predict the outcome in terms of price and output of a change in one of these variables.

The effects of changes in supply and demand are clearly presented in figures 2/7a and 2/7b.

These are:

- an increase in demand will lead in the short term to higher prices and higher quantities demanded: i.e. a movement in prices initially from OP_O to OP_H as producers cannot respond immediately to the change in demand then settling back to OP_N as production responds and the quantity demanded increases from OQ_O to OQ_N as shown in figure 2/7a;
- the long term result depends on the long term pattern of production and the extent to which the increased demand is sustained and is therefore harder to predict, but may lead to increased quantity supplied for little or no increase in the "real" price;
- a decrease in demand is likely to have the opposite effect, all other things being held the same
- increases in supply lead to lower prices and increased demand as in figure 2/7b where demand increases to OQ_N and price falls to OP_N.
- shortages in supply lead to price rises and reduced demand;

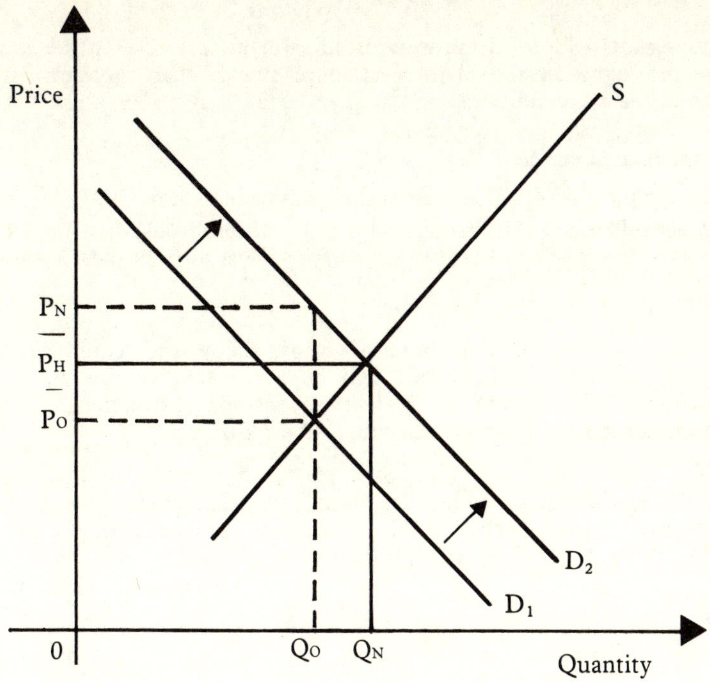

Fig. 2/7a

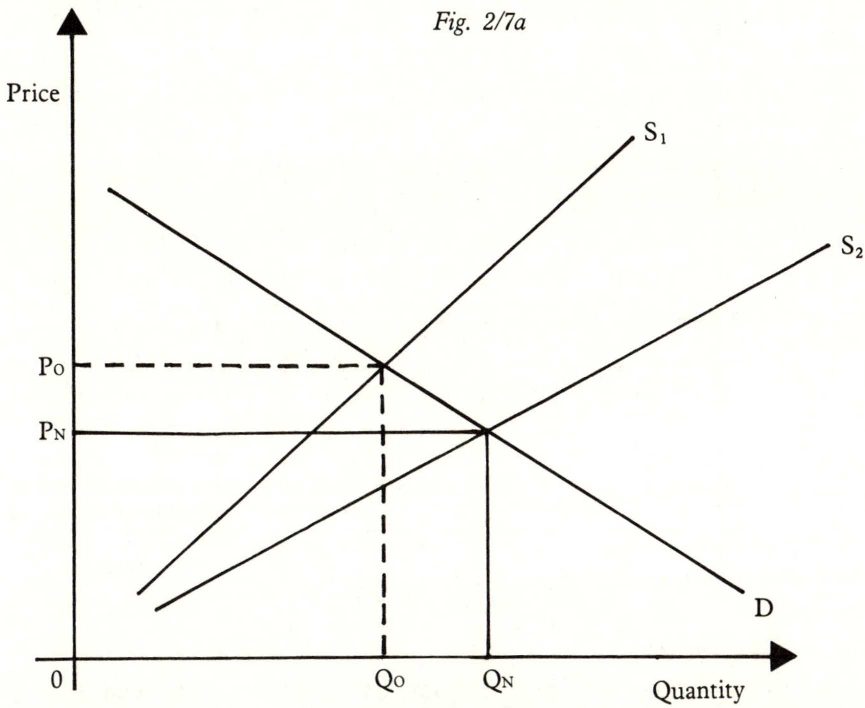

Fig. 2/7b

It is important to note the process of adjustment that takes place and observe that consumers tend to react more quickly than producers to changes in market conditions.

5.3.2 External interference

A further application of these tools is the example of external interference in the market by means of the imposition of either minimum or maximum price controls, practical examples of which exist in the agricultural policies of the E.E.C. Figure 2/8 summarises the effect of such policies which are as follows:

a) if a maximum price is imposed below the market equilibrium (OP_{MAX}) the ensuing result will be a shortfall in the official markets (WX) leading to the development of black markets. This experience is commonly associated with rationing;

b) if a minimum price is imposed above the market equilibrium (OP_{MIN}) the result will be overproduction (YZ) and surpluses such as have resulted in the E.E.C. It should be noted that the U.S.A. has also suffered from this problem.

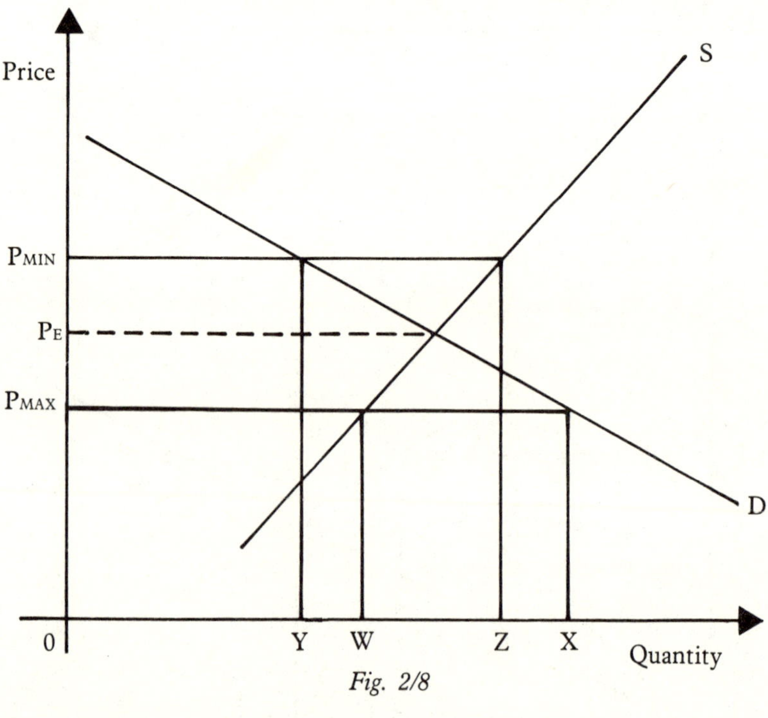

Fig. 2/8

6.0 Elasticity

We have seen that the interaction of the forces of supply and demand determine the price level at which goods will be traded. The respective curves also indicate how responsive consumers and producers are to **changes** in price. This measure of responsiveness to changes in price or other variables is referred to in economics as **elasticity.** Thus the responsiveness of consumers is known as the **Elasticity of Demand** and that of producers is referred to as the **Elasticity of Supply.** As we have already indicated demand is usually more elastic than supply. The reasons will be examined below.

The degree of elasticity can be measured by comparing the change in price to the change in the quantity supplied or demanded. It is therefore calculated by comparing percentage changes in price and quantity as a means of comparison according to a common denominator. The general formula is normally expressed as:

$$\frac{\text{percentage change in the dependent variable}}{\text{percentage change in the independent variable}}$$

where dependent variable is quantity demanded or supplied;

independent variable can be price, income or another variable.

Note: the independent variable is changed and the effect on the dependent variable is observed.

6.1 Elasticity of Demand

Elasticity of demand - i.e. the response of the quantity demanded - can be examined with respect to changes in:

* price - **price elasticity,** where the independent variable is the price of the good or service;
* income - **income elasticity,** where the income of the consumer is the independent variable;
* prices of other goods - **cross elasticity,** where the prices of other goods are the independent variables.

6.1.1 Price elasticitv

As the changes in price and quantity will usually be in opposite directions, the resulting price elasticity value is negative. The negative sign has been omitted from in table 2/1 as this does not interfere with the interpretation of results. For practical purposes we shall summarise only the interpretation and application of the co-efficients of elasticity with values greater than zero and less than infinity:

Value	Terminology	Meaning
<1	relatively inelastic	change in quantity is less than the change in price
$=1$	unit elasticity	change in quantity equal to the change in price
>1	relatively elastic	change in quantity greater than the change in price

6.1.1.1 The determinants of price elasticity

The various factors influencing the extent to which consumers respond to changes in price have been identified as:

- **the existence of close substitutes:** the greater the level of competition, the greater the degree of elasticity;
- **the price of the good in relation to the consumers income:** consumers are obviously more sensitive to price changes in goods and services which command a significant proportion of their budget;
- **the range of possible uses or the degree of necessity:** greater flexibility of use of a product will reduce its sensitivity to price rises;
- **advertising and brand loyalty;**
- **the degree of necessity:** basic products will continue to be consumed as price rises. This is usually explained in terms of foodstuffs etc., but can equally apply to situations where the mere participation in an activity enforces the purchase of a certain product - e.g. car ownership and insurance. Many corollaries can be found in the business environment.

6.1.1.2 Applications of price elasticity

An ability to predict consumer response to changes in price is of value to:

- **manufacturers** in attempting to forecast the revenue effect of price increases or reductions;
- **Chancellor of Exchequer** in determining the effect on tax revenues of changes in tax rates;
- **importers/exporters** when determining the effect of a change in the value of the currency.

6.1.2 Income elasticity

The independent variable in this instance is consumers' income, which is usually understood to represent "real" income or purchasing power rather than simply money income a rise in which does not necessarily leave consumers better off. A rise in the level of income is therefore perceived as an increase in the material standard of living.

The value of income elasticity is calculated in the manner described above and generally speaking, goods with a value of 1 or greater are known as "normal" goods, i.e. demand rises with income, whereas goods with a value of less than 1 - i.e. demand falls or remains constant as incomes increase - are known as "inferior" goods.

The income elasticity value assigned to good is not absolute, it changes over time, particularly as an economy develops and increases are experienced in the material standard of living. Increased economic development is associated with the following trends:

- increased application of mass production techniques, and the consequential higher capital values at risk as well as increased stock values and business interruption costs;
- the increase in the scale of the service sector with concomitant implications for the development of liability and indemnity risk;
- the growth of the multi-national organisation of production and the increased risks of interdependent world-wide productive facilities, together with the unavoidable increased risks of losses arising from movements in exchange risks (exchange risk);
- the demands of increased economic growth have placed visible and short-term irreversible effects upon the world's resources which have led to pressure for the amelioration of the effects of pollution on and conservation of the environment.

6.1.3 Cross elasticity

This measures the effect of changes in the prices of other goods on the demand of the goods under observation. It is calculated as indicated in section 6.0 above. The main conclusions to note are that if the co-efficient of cross elasticity is negative then the goods in question are complementary; if it is positive they are substitutes or competitive goods. For instance, examples of complementary goods would be cars and petrol, house mortgages and life assurance endowment policies or microcomputers and floppy disks whereas examples of substitute goods would be butter and margarine, rail and coach travel or comprehensive and third party motor insurance cover.

6.2 Elasticity of Supply

We can measure suppliers responsiveness to changes in price in the same manner as for consumers. The range of values is similar to those calculated for price elasticity of demand. The factors which influence suppliers ability to respond to changes in price are:

- **the length of the production cycle;** the shorter the production period the more elastic the response to price changes;
- **stock levels:** against the ability to respond quickly to changes in prices or product demand most be balanced the additional costs of sufficient stocks and consequently the additional values at risk
- **the range of products and/or markets in which the producer is operating;** this also has implications for level of stocks etc.;
- **availability of the factors of production:** shortages can lead either to reduced output or higher costs as producers are forced to bid for a restricted pool of resources;
- **the costs of entry to and exit from the market:** i.e. market research, training, "tooling-up" etc.;
- **nature of contractual commitments:** which restrict freedom of action.

7.0 Demand Re-visited

The explanation of consumer choice and preference is based on the **theory of utility** which seeks to explain human choice in terms of the "satisfaction" or utility that is derived from consumption of goods and services. Although measurement of utility is not actually possible, the concept is sufficiently powerful to provide a plausible explanation of consumer behaviour.

7.1 Concepts of Utility

The following concepts are important to an appreciation of the theory and should therefore be studied carefully:

- **total utility** * the total satisfaction that is derived from consumption by the individual and aggregates the utility derived from the purchases undertaken over a period of time;
- **marginal utility** * the additional amount of utility derived from the consumption of an additional unit of the good;
- **the hypothesis of diminishing marginal utility** * the assumption is made that the additional unit consumed will *always* have a lower contribution to total utility than the previous one.

The relationship between the quantity consumed and these concepts can be depicted graphically as in figures 2/9a and 2/9b.

Utility theory is useful as an explanation of why, beyond a certain point, consumption will cease - even in the case of a "free" good. It recognises that consumers value different products differently, and thereby provides a rationale of trade between individuals. Its conclusions and predictions about economic behaviour are used to explain the nature of the relationship between price and quantity demanded, furnishing a theoretical basis for the construction of the demand curve.

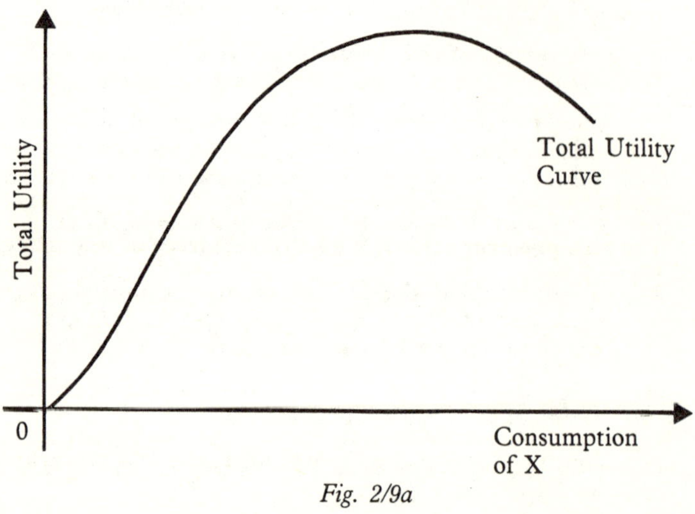

Fig. 2/9a

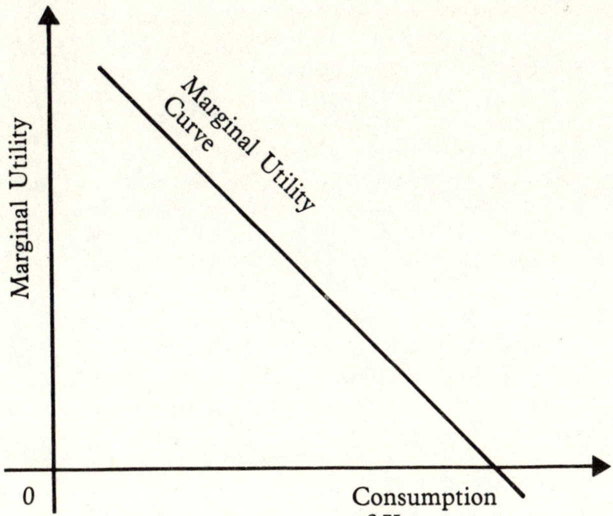

Fig. 2/9b

7.2 **Utility Theory and Risk Aversion**

The concept of utility has been employed to explain the nature of insurance purchasing. The basis of the explanation lies in risk attitudes which can vary from person to person. People's attitudes to risk fall into one of three categories:

i) risk neutral

ii) risk preference

iii) risk aversion.

The **risk neutral** person exhibits a reaction to risk in line with its statistical probability. The reduction in his utility caused by the existence of risk is directly in line with the likelihood of its occurrence. This is shown by line OB in Figure 2/10.

The **risk preferer** actually enjoys the existence of risk and uncertainty. His satisfaction is heightened in its presence. In contrast to the normal position the risk preferer experiences increasing marginal utility as a result of the chance of loss, and the greater the values at risk, the greater the level of utility. Hence the curve OY.

The **risk averter** exhibits the more normal reaction to risk, that is he is intimidated by it. The reduction in utility in the presence of uncertainty is greater than the statistical probabilities if its occurrence. This is represented by the curve OR.

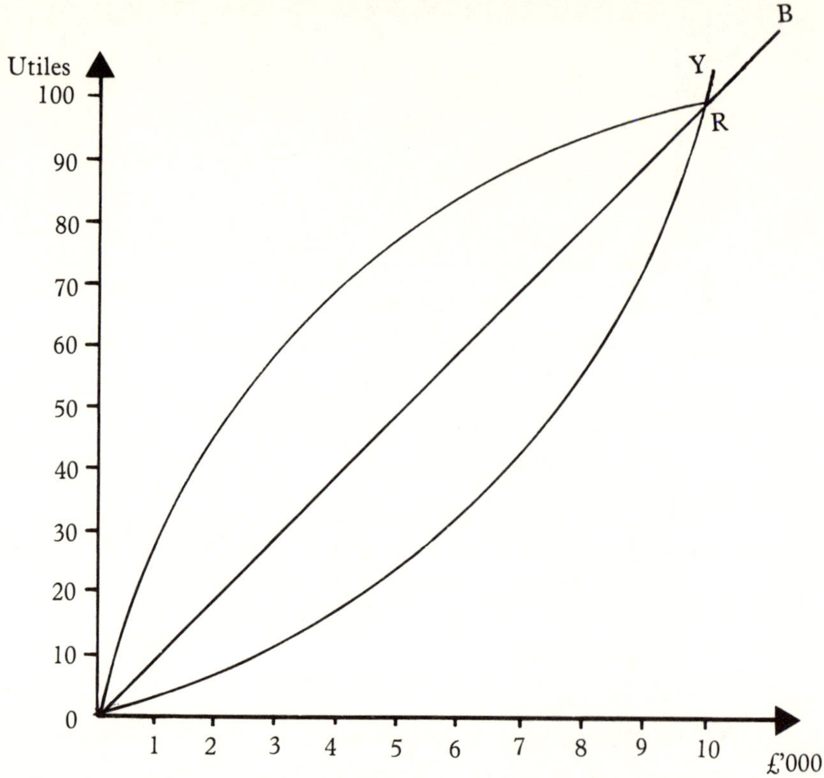

Fig. 2/10

The benefit of identifying this behaviour is the understanding of insurance purchasing decisions and predictions about buying behaviour that can be made.

For example:

Car valued at £10,000, when owned and driven by an 18 year old is subject to a 10% chance of write-off.

The expected value of the car owners wealth can be calculated:

$$W_2 \times p + W_1(1-p)$$

where W_2 is the wealth under a no loss situation
W_1 is wealth after a loss has occurred
p is the probability of no loss occurring
$(1-p)$ is the probability of loss

In this example it is £9000, try it for yourself.

This however only reflects the statistical probabilities which as we have noted are insufficient to explain a persons reaction to risk. The impact on utility has therefore to be calculated, thus:

$$U(W_2) \times p + U(W_1)(1-p)$$

The utility values assigned to the levels of wealth therefore become crucial to the analysis. Drawing on the above example the situation can be represented on Figure 2/11 below.

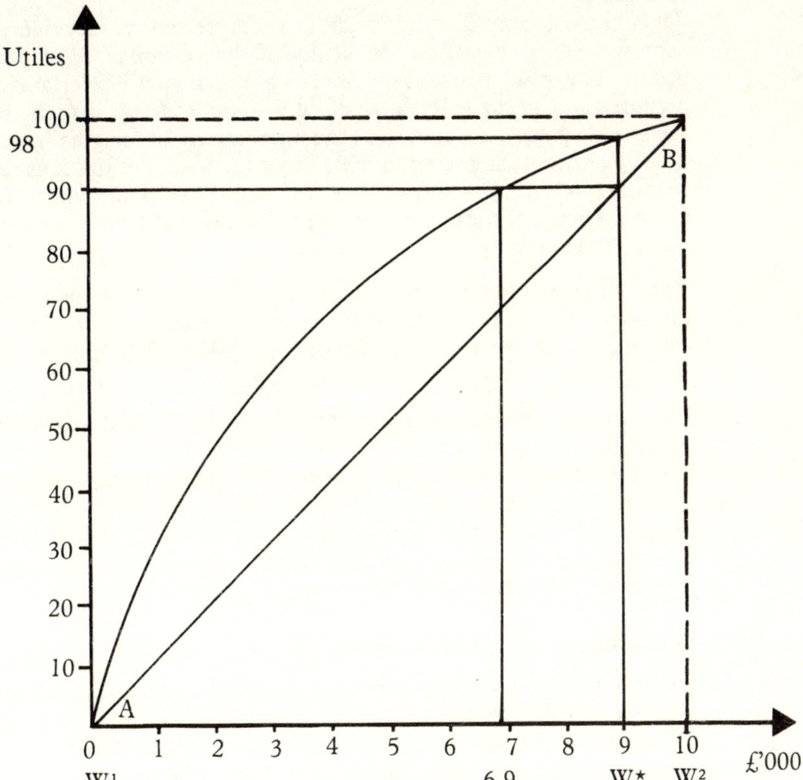

Fig. 2/11

We can assume that full use of the car (W_2) yields 100 units of utility and that a write-off (W_1) will reduce this to zero. W* is the expected value of wealth. The expected level of utility based on these figures is 90 utiles.

From the graph it can be seen that the risk averse individual's utility has been affected by the existence of uncertainty. Contrasted with that of the risk neutral person (90 utiles) the value placed on the value of wealth by the risk averter is greater (98 utiles). This however only applies when this level of wealth is certain; that is, 98 utiles only corresponds to a guaranteed figure of £9000. The point is that this figure is not guaranteed because the conditions of uncertainty still obtain.

The difference between the risk averter and the neutrally risk person is that the former will be willing to pay more than the expected loss to exchange uncertainty for certainty. The risk averter compares a position of uncertainty with one of certainty. Certainty could be made available in the form of a financial guarantee that if the loss occurred, the full value of wealth would be restored. This guarantee would have a cost. The extent to which the consumer is prepared to pay for this guarantee in excess of the expected loss is the measure of the risk aversion of the consumer.

Thus in our example under conditions of uncertainty, represented by the expected value of wealth, the utility of the consumer is reduced to 90 utiles. The risk averse consumer would far prefer certainty and is prepared to pay for it in the form of a payment to an insurer. In return the insurer guarantees to restore the purchaser to his original position W_2. The payment of the premium will reduce the wealth of the consumer. The consumer will prepared to reduce his wealth to a point where the utility derived from certainty is the same as that derived from uncertainty - 90 utiles in this example.

Thus we can reiterate our conclusion stated above that the amount paid in excess of the expected loss is a measurement of the extent of the consumers risk aversion - £3,100 (i.e. £10,000 - £6,900) in our example, as depicted in the individual's utility curve.

In conclusion, the complexity of individual human and group behaviour makes it unlikely at the moment that utility schedules could be derived in order that an analysis could be conducted in the manner outlined above, however the benefits of this form of analysis is that it points up the necessary trade-off between the costs and benefits of certainty in an uncertain world and permits a closer examination of the factors influencing the risk financing decision.

8.0 Summary and Conclusion

In this introductory chapter to the economic environment, we saw that the basic economic problem was one of finite resources - referred to as the factors of production - and unlimited wants. We noted that one of the means that had developed to deal with the allocative problems posed by this dilemma was the price mechanism which was the basis for the system known as the market economy. It was claimed that this mechanism was relatively successful as it was the basis on which the economic behaviour of many highly complex modern economies was founded, coordinating millions of separate decisions in order to provide consumers with goods which they wanted to buy, in the quantities they required when they wanted. We saw that not all such decisions are left to the market, that in some instances government intervened and acted as a provider of goods and services.

Prices, we saw, were determined by the forces of supply and demand in the market place and noted that basic framework of analysis could be applied to other markets in which the firm was operating.

We looked in particular at the market for goods and services and discovered the factors which led to the demand for a specific good. We also analysed the theory of consumer choice and discovered that its basis - utility theory - could be adapted to analyse the impact of risk aversion on the insurance purchasing decision.

Next we examined the factors determining the supply of a product and noted that these may often restrict the suppliers ability to respond to changes in price.

The degree of responsiveness to changes in price on the part of producers or consumers was identified as the elasticity of supply and the elasticity of demand respectively.

The presumption of this chapter has been the case that an appreciation of basic economic analytical tools will enable analysis of markets other than those considered in this chapter, and can effectively contribute to the formulation of risk management policies which support, and in some cases anticipate, the commercial activities of the firm.

Chapter Three

THE ECONOMIC ENVIRONMENT — Production and Costs

1.0 Key Points

Turning from the product markets we shall now concentrate on the factors determining the supply of goods and services provided by the firm.

The purpose of this chapter will be:

- to examine the nature and behaviour of the costs and revenues of the business enterprise;
- to examine the various forms of market condition that a firm may operate under and observe the influence of these on the decision to supply;
- to appreciate the contribution that is made by risk management in this area;
- to provide a framework for analysis of the commercial activities of the firm for the risk manager;
- to identify the support that the risk manager can provide to general management in the production, distribution and marketing of the firms products;

2.0 Production and Costs

A market is where buyers and sellers meet. The marketplace may be physical or electronic, local or national. Its purpose is to allow the interaction of the forces of supply and demand as described in the previous chapter. As we have already indicated the producer operates in a number of different markets, which can broadly be described as **resource** and **product** markets. The relationship between these two types of market is illustrated overleaf in figure 3/1.

In the last chapter the basic motivation for supply was identified as profit. Whilst this may be the reason for production taking place, the quantity that is eventually supplied is determined by that costs that have to be borne by the firm. We noted in chapter 3 that the economic concept of cost refers to the rewards that have to be paid to the factors of production, including entrepreneurs, for the use of their services.

2.1 Costs

Costs can be classified as:

- **fixed** or **variable,** which describes their behaviour in the short term in relation to output (figure 3/2a). The short term is defined as the period during which the quantity of at least one of the factors cannot be changed. This factor is referred to as the fixed factor because it remains unchanged over a particular range of output. The

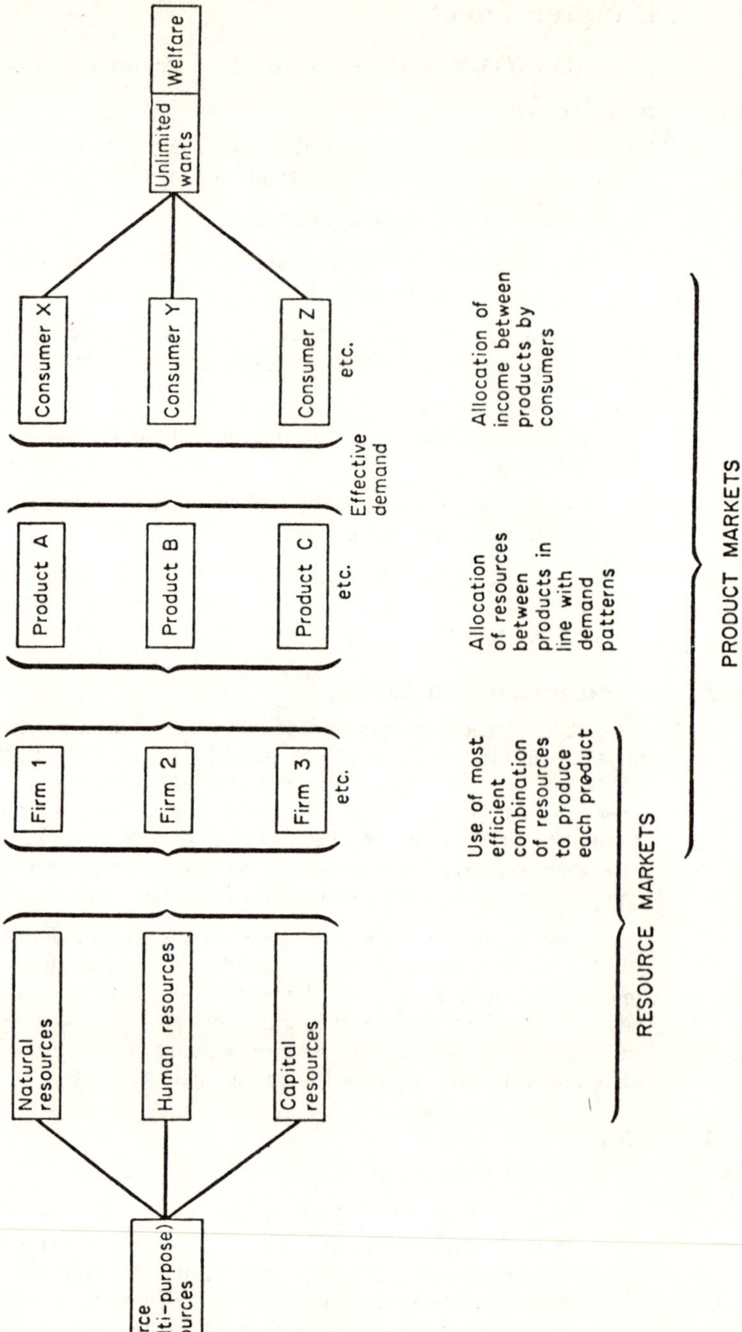
Scarce (multi-purpose) resources
Natural resources
Human resources
Capital resources
Firm 1
Firm 2
Firm 3
etc.
Product A
Product B
Product C
etc.
Effective demand
Consumer X
Consumer Y
Consumer Z
etc.
Unlimited wants
Welfare
Use of most efficient combination of resources to produce each product
Allocation of resources between products in line with demand patterns
Allocation of income between products by consumers
RESOURCE MARKETS
PRODUCT MARKETS

Fig. 3/1

amount of the variable factor employed changes over the same range of output. The long term is defined as a period during which the quantity of all factors is free to vary.

Fixed costs are attributable to the fixed factor and variable costs to the variable factor;

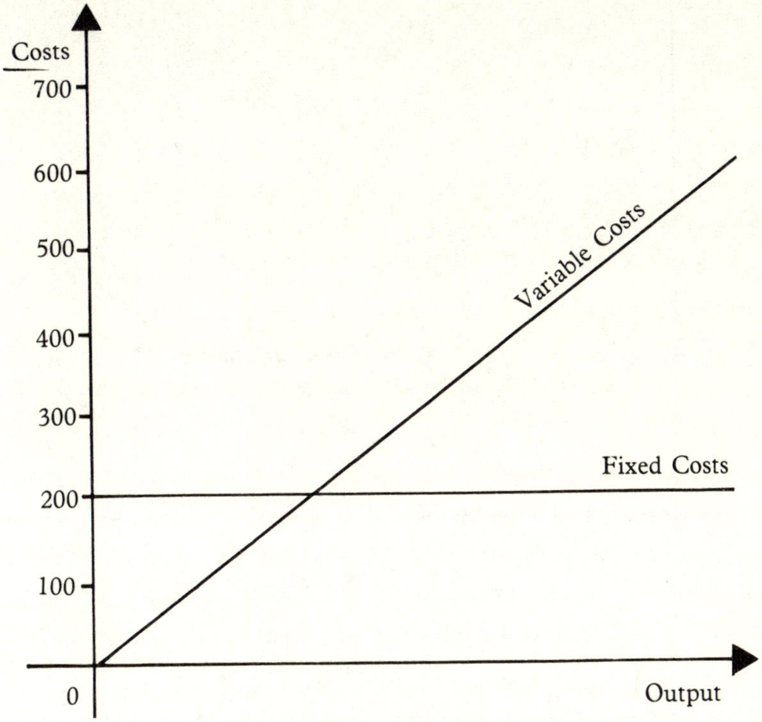

Fig. 3/2a

– **average** or **marginal,** which measure the relationship of total costs in relation to output and the relationship between additional costs attributable to additional output respectively (figure 3/2b).

Average and marginal costs are calculated as follows:

$$\text{AVERAGE COST} = \frac{\text{total costs}}{\text{total output}}$$

$$= \text{cost per unit}$$

$$\text{MARGINAL COST} = \frac{\text{change in total costs}}{\text{change in total output}}$$

$$= \text{additional cost per additional unit of output}$$

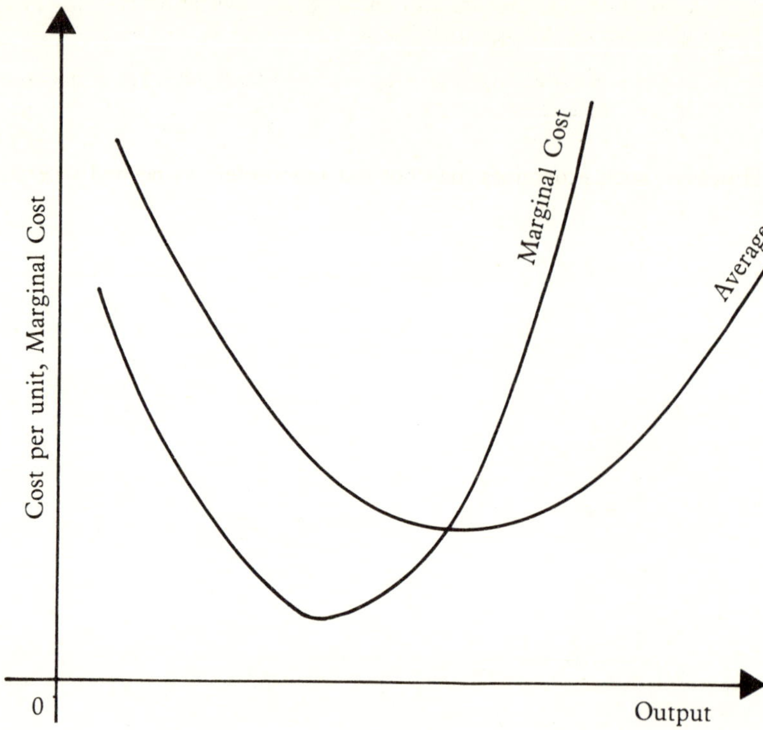

Fig. 3/2b

Average costs are influenced by both fixed and variable costs, whereas marginal costs are solely the function of the relationship between variable costs and additional output. The relationship between average and marginal costs is important because of the general predictions that can be made about behaviour of costs. Generally speaking, the marginal costs will always be less than average costs when average costs are falling, but will be greater than average costs when these are rising. This implies that the point of intersection of these costs will be when average cost reaches its minimum level. Marginal costs however will have already 'bottomed-out' and will be on the increase when this point occurs.

Returns to scale, often termed the 'economies of large scale production', arise because of the benefits of increasing the amount of the 'fixed' factor. This however does not occur as frequently as changes in the variable factor - hence the terminology. It normally involves capital expenditure, such changes being made in the 'long-term' in distinction to the short-term when these factors are usually fixed. It is conventional to regard labour as an example of the variable factor and machinery (or capital) as an example of the fixed factor. Increases in the quantity of the fixed factor will only be undertaken if by doing so the producer can reduce the level of unit or average costs. These savings may often be possible as a direct result of the larger scale of production, since larger scale will lead to greater technical and organisational efficiency, marketing and financing economies and savings in raw material and other costs through discounts available on bulk purchasing. The result of successive increases in scale to access these savings will be lower average costs at higher levels of output, as illustrated in figure 3/3. The economies of large scale production are the economic justification for mass production techniques.

However, such economies may not last indefinitely as beyond a certain scale of operation management and industrial problems increase disproportionately. This is the reason for the increase in the long-run average cost curve beyond the minimum efficient scale in figure 3/3.

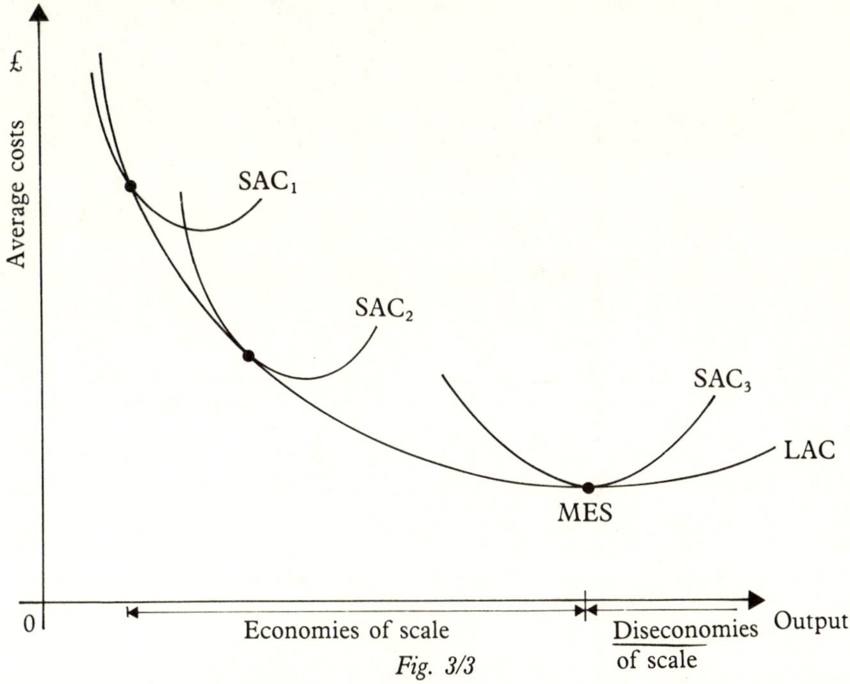

Fig. 3/3

Key:
LAC: Long run average cost curve
SAC_1, SAC_2, SAC_3: Short run average cost curves at different levels of fixed factor
MES: Minimum efficient scale

2.2 Revenue

Revenue can be classified as total, average and marginal. These are defined as follows:

TOTAL REVENUE = total number of units sold × price

AVERAGE REVENUE $= \dfrac{\text{total revenue}}{\text{no. of units sold}}$

= price

MARGINAL REVENUE = $\frac{\text{change in total revenue}}{\text{change in no. of units sold}}$

= additional revenue from each extra unit sold

Their behaviour is depicted in figures 3/4a and 3/4b.

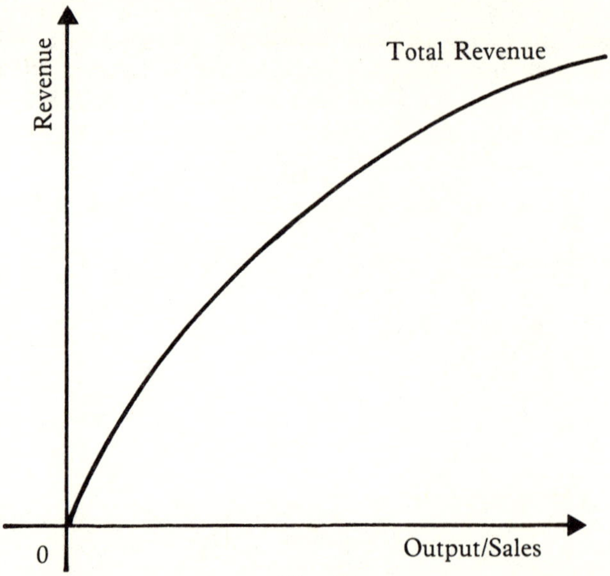

Fig. 3/4a

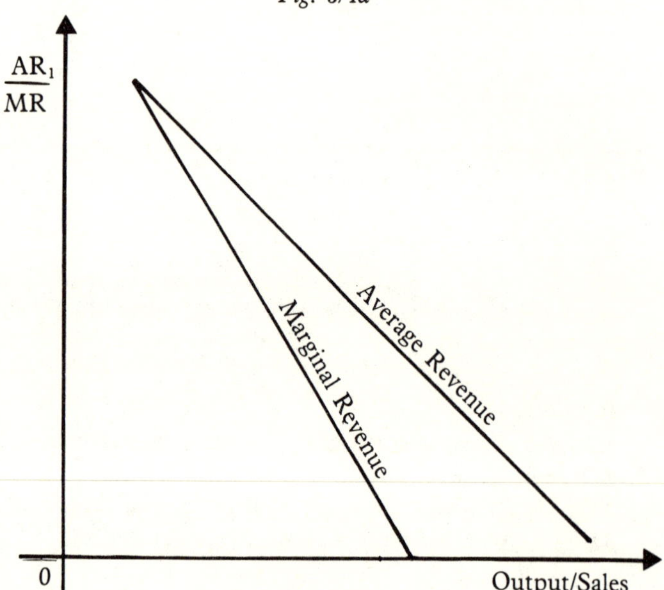

Fig. 3/4b

2.3 Profit Maximisation

The revenue and cost curves can be combined on the same diagram to determine the output and price at which the producer is willing to supply. Economists assume that the desire to maximise profits is common to all producers. Although this may not fully reflect the range of factors that influence the producer, it is a useful working rule which is straightforward to apply. All decisions of producers are therefore based on this criterion. Once this point has been reached the producer will have no desire to change either output or price - he will be in **equilibrium.**

The point of maximum profit and therefore of equilibrium occurs when marginal revenue equals marginal cost — that is, where MR = MC at output OA and price OR in figure 3/5.

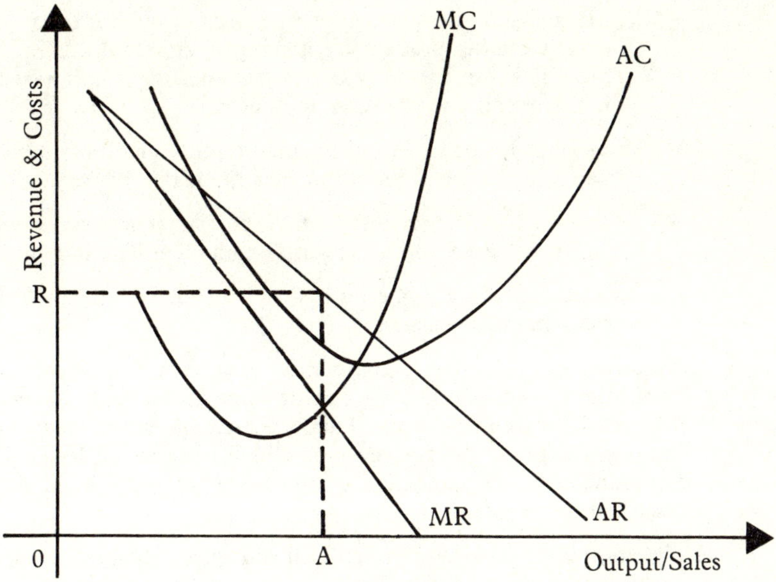

Fig. 3/5

This means that the additional revenue generated from the sale of the last unit of output is equal to the costs associated with its production. To expand output beyond this level would result in a reduction in profit because with marginal cost increasing and marginal revenue on the decrease the costs will exceed the revenue from the marginal unit produced and sold. This rule applies no matter the market conditions under which the firm is operating.

3.0 Market Conditions

This refers to the institutional arrangements within the market place. There are two basic types of market structure:

- the perfect market
- imperfect markets.

Imperfect markets can be further subdivided into those of monopoly, duopoly, oligopoly and monopolistic competition.

The degree of competition in the market will determine the pricing and output decisions of the producer. We can now examine the behaviour of producers under these various conditions.

3.1 Perfect Competition

The conditions for perfect competition are:

- a large number of buyers and sellers: this means that no single producer or consumer is large enough to influence the price in the market;
- homogeneous products: in other words no producer can influence demand for his product by making it appear different from any other. The implication of this is that consumers will have no cause for preferring one producer to another;
- free entry to and exit from the market: this condition is particularly related to the development or decline of the market;
- there are no transport costs - i.e. no barriers to movement within the market by either consumers or factors of production;
- perfect knowledge, where all participants have full knowledge of all prices etc in the market.

Producers in the perfectly competitive market are therefore said to be 'price-takers', because nothing can be done to mitigate the controlling effect of the price mechanism. They are therefore at the mercy of market forces as the price (average revenue) which rules for all levels of sales is determined by the interaction of the forces of supply and demand as described in an earlier chapter.

This form of market is highly artificial and extremely rare. It is structured in this manner to exclude all other influences apart from price but does however permit certain conclusions to be drawn about market behaviour. Once these have been derived, the effects of easing these restrictive conditions can be observed.

The consequences of perfect competition for economic behaviour are as follows:

i) when AR > MC, (figure 3/6a) the firm is said to be earning *super normal profits*. These however are only available in the short term as others firms are attracted to the industry and these profits are competed away;

ii) firms earning less than *normal profits* (AR < MC in figure 3/6b) will leave the industry to seek more profitable opportunities elsewhere as they are not restrained from leaving by high set-up costs etc. Since all firms do not trade under the same cost conditions, those less efficient higher cost firms will be the first to leave the industry;

iii) the *long-run* the position of the industry will be one of *normal profits* where MR = MC = AR = AC as in figure 3/6c).

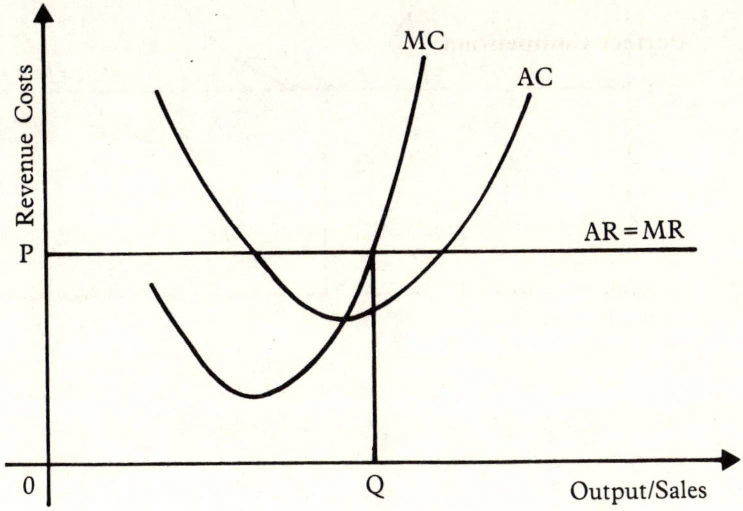

Fig. 3/6a

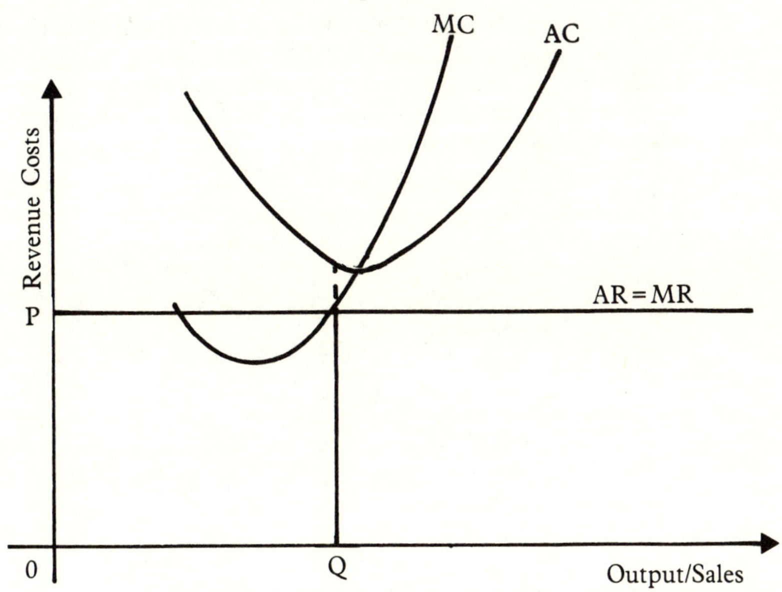

Fig. 3/6b

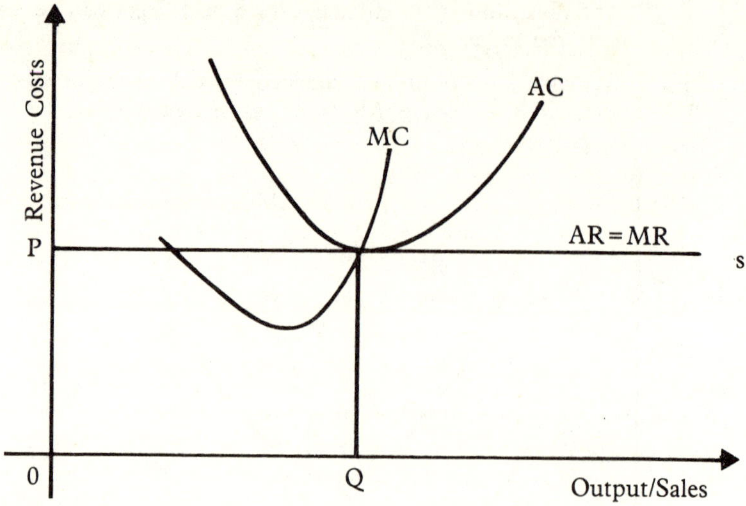

Fig. 3/6c

3.2 Monopoly

Monopoly is the opposite of perfect competition, in that there is a single producer (or a number producers acting as one - 'cartel') in the market place. Consumers now have no choice with the result that the monopolist becomes a 'price-maker' in contrast to the producer in the perfectly competitive market. In addition entry to the market is restricted either by natural forces, the monopolist or an outside body like the state. In

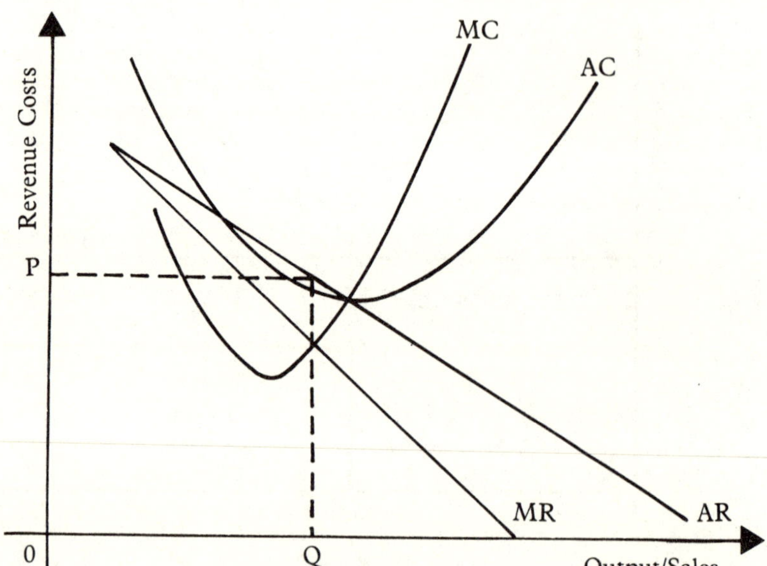

Fig. 3/7

practical terms any firm in the U.K. with a market share of more than 25% is described by the state as a monopolist. This definition has been set by UK. government as part of its machinery of legislative control over monopolies.

The monopolist remains subject to the law of demand and cannot control both price and output. He therefore faces a downward sloping average revenue curve. This allows the outcome illustrated in figure 3/7 to exist.

The economic consequences of monoply are:

i) the profit maximisation point occurs where AR > AC and *super-normal* or monopoly profits are earned. They are referred to as monopoly profits because unlike perfect competition they can be sustained in the long run by virtue of the monopolist's position as sole producer;

ii) the monopolist will normally charge a higher price for a lower output than would be the case under perfect competition;

iii) as sole producer the monopolist may be able to exercise *price discrimination* by selling the same goods to different groups of consumers. This will normally only be successful if the markets can be kept separate and consumers prevented from buying in one and selling in another

iv) since production does not continue to the point of lowest average costs this represents a waste of resources.

For these reasons monopolies are either usually discouraged or controlled in developed economies. They may be permitted to exist if this is seen to be in the public interest. Such examples may in the provision of social infrastructure, to reduce the effects of wasteful competition, to protect an industry from external competition because the domestic economy is insufficient to support more than one or two producers, and to encourage an industry to undertake substantial research and development expenditure which would have national benefit.

3.3 Monopolistic Competition

Similar to perfect competition but where all goods are not alike, it is marked by product differentiation. The result for the producer is that like the monopolist he now faces his own demand curve, the elasticity of which depends on the degree of similarity between his and his competitors goods. Unlike the monopolist however he is unable to prevent other firms entering the industry if the product is profitable. The outcome in this instance is as depicted in figure 3/8.

The monopolistically competitive market will display the following features:

i) an importance placed on product differentiation;

ii) *super-normal profits* in the short term as the result of the element of differentiation;

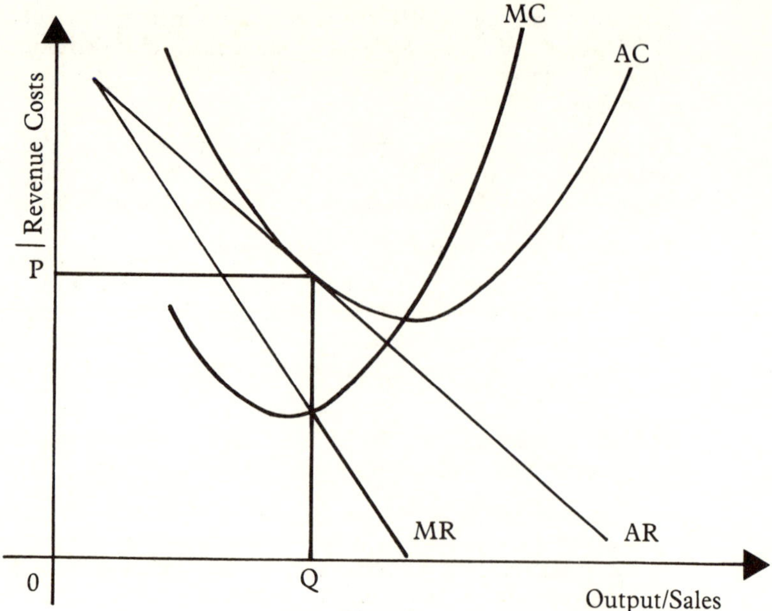

Fig. 3/8

iii) a long run position of *normal profits* as more firms enter the industry producing similar goods and forcing a reduction in price as a result of the reduction in demand;

iv) although the firm is now only earning normal profits it is still not producing at the optimal level of output to minimise unit costs that is where MR = MC and AR = AC but AR > MC and therefore represents a less than fully efficient utilisation of the factors available.

3.4 Oligopoly

Or competition among the few. The conditions of oligopoly are those of a small number of producers commanding a substantial proportion of market share. High barriers to entry such as advertising and set-up costs are usually associated with such conditions.

Oligopoly tends to manifest itself in the following manner:

- high barriers to entry to the market, usually reinforced by high marketing/advertising costs;
- a tendency for firms to act together, whether formally or informally;
- very little price competition;
- influential in the factor markets since as principal consumers of factor services they can affect the market price, higher costs being passed on to consumers.

4.0 Distribution

Determination of the market is however only the first part of the task of management. Once the strategy, product range and market has been agreed the process of producing the goods to the required specification and distributing them to wholesale and retail outlets must begin. Although market analysis is normally associated with the commercial management of the business the risk manager is also involved at many of the other stages including:

- production - the protection of materials, plant, machinery, buildings and labour force;
- the protection of stock;
- warehousing - buildings, goods and personnel;
- transportation.

Each of the above stages in the bringing of the product to the marketplace is fraught with pure risk as the assets of the business are exposed to the risks of fire, flood, theft, breakdown etc each of which is within the province of the risk manager. The picture is further complicated by the fact that different stages of the production process may be carried out on premises in different locations, that finished goods may be stored under differing conditions and the provision of goods and services may be provided across national boundaries. Furthermore the company may incur liability as the result of injuries suffered by its employees or damage caused by its products. The position is summarised in the diagram overleaf reproduced from the *Handbook of Risk Management.*

5.0 Summary and Conclusions

In this chapter we have examined the decision of the producer to supply under differing theoretical market conditions. We recognised that these models could not duplicate the complexities of the real world, but argued for their use on the grounds of the insight they provide to the behaviour of producers in the market place and the facility they offer for the prediction of the effect of changes in the system.

Risk management applications of these concepts could include the following:

- an appreciation of the variable and fixed loss components in loss reduction expenditures;
- an awareness of the nature of the market conditions in the various areas in which the the organisation is operating i.e. whether they could be classified as oligopolistic or monopolistically competitive. In some cases the firm may be a monopolist in terms of the legislative description.
- The importance of this is to appreciate the competitive pressures under which the firm is operating. Cost minimisation is an effective and valid means towards the achievement of profit maximisation. The risk managers hand may then be strengthened in these

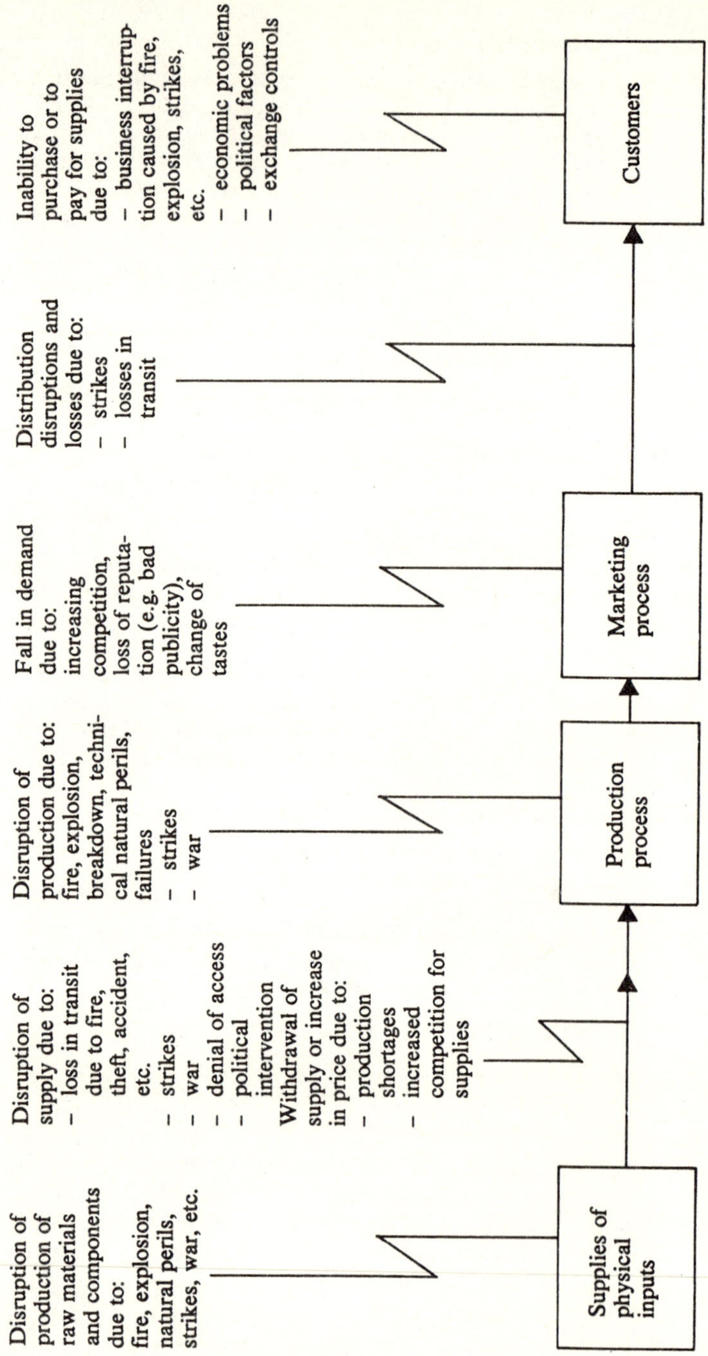

Disruption of production of raw materials and components due to: fire, explosion, natural perils, strikes, war, etc.
Disruption of supply due to:
– loss in transit due to fire, theft, accident, etc.
– strikes
– war
– denial of access
– political intervention
Withdrawal of supply or increase in price due to:
– production shortages
– increased competition for supplies
Disruption of production due to: fire, explosion, breakdown, technical natural perils, failures
– strikes
– war
Fall in demand due to: increasing competition, loss of reputation (e.g. bad publicity), change of tastes
Distribution disruptions and losses due to:
– strikes
– losses in transit
Inability to purchase or to pay for supplies due to:
– business interruption caused by fire, explosion, strikes, etc.
– economic problems
– political factors
– exchange controls
Supplies of physical inputs
Production process
Marketing process
Customers

Fig. 3/9

circumstances if he can demonstrate that his contribution does in fact lead to the achievement of this goal. As mentioned in section 3.1 the lowest cost firm can earn super-normal profits for the longest period.

An ability to read conditions in the market place may permit a wider perspective on changing market conditions. For instance the pattern of insurance market cycles can be can be predicted from economic theory. If the return from insurance and related activities is sufficient additional capacity is attracted to the market place. This is seen initially and principally in reinsurance market but the effects do not take long in making themselves felt in the direct market. If demand remains static in the short term the increase in capacity leads to a fall in price. The consequences are that in the short term buyers benefit from lower premiums, wider terms of cover or both. Eventually however the lower prices produce returns that are not sufficient for some suppliers to remain in the market. Less efficient or committed operators leave the market as profitability declines. With capacity and competition reduced, the remaining suppliers are able to charge higher prices thus leading to 'hardening of the market'. All these changes are predictable from basic economic theory. The timing and fine detail cannot be supplied from the basic theory however, that is the province of the practitioners of economic analysis.

on this occasion due to the absence of certain institutional factors that had previously been in place) and will not be the last either. The timing and fine detail cannot be supplied from the basic theory, that is the province of the practicioners of economic analysis.

- the importance of revenue generating activities or assets can be more fully appreciated. Again the degree of market competition sets the impact of the loss within its context, the greater the degree of competition the greater the need for protection of the vital assets. This is especially important to grasp because risk reduction and control expenditure is particularly vulnerable to pruning when a firm is experiencing severe competitive conditions.
- finally, the risk manager could become aware of the different markets in which the firm operates in both consumer and factor markets bringing the process of risk management to bear on the risks encountered in these areas. Each facet of the organisation's operations could be examined within this framework. Some risks may be unique to particular markets or processes others may exist throughout all operations. From this analysis a central view can be taken.

Producers are also active in the markets for the resources, the demand for which is based on the demand for goods and services in the product markets, and is constrained by availability of the relevant factors, mobility of the factors, the method of production i.e. the mix of factors and any changes initiated by the technological developments and the efficiency of the factors. Since the producer is attempting to derive maximum efficiency in the usage of resources, the combination or mix of factors chosen should represent the best available under the constraints placed by the prevailing technology. Loss of productive capacity through fire, flood, breakdown or accident etc. will therefore frustrate this purpose. Since the profitability of the enterprise depends on the income-generating ability of these assets it will be important that production downtime be reduced to a minimum. The contribution of the risk manager in this area is obvious.

Furthermore, changes in technology lead to changes in the combination of the factors, which apart from the industrial relations risk, gives rise to others within the remit of the risk manager. The risks arising from new processes and new machinery may be unknown but still have to be shouldered by the company if it is to make use of these developments. The capital at risk in newer technology is often of a higher value and the extent of damage caused by breakdown or failure, whether this be accidental or deliberate, may also be more widespread. The management of such changes must also include those responsible for its operation and those displaced by its implementation. The need for protection and security becomes apparent under these circumstances.

Finally, we noted the process by which the reward to labour was determined. The role fulfilled by the risk manager in this area is firstly that of protection of these resources, but it has also been suggested that effective risk management may also have a part to play in the industrial relations environment. Labour may place a sufficient premium of the benefits of asset protection to be prepared to include it in the collective bargaining process, whilst employers may view the same benefits as part of the overall package of rewards offered to the labour force.

Chapter Four

THE ECONOMIC ENVIRONMENT — The Domestic Economy

1.0 Introduction

The foregoing analysis and discussion has concentrated on the activities of the individual firm or industry. Passing reference was made to forces outwith the control of the individual firm but to which it had to respond. As we have indicated in the above section the aim in this chapter is to look at the wider picture, identify the components of the modern economy and note how these interact. The individual firm is part of a larger scenario and therefore has a contribution to make to the economic health and welfare of the nation. The nation itself is greater than the sum of the parts because there are a number of activities peculiar to the state separate from those of its citizens and the means of wealth creation. The nature of the relationship between the state and its citizens reflects the cultural and political climate of the nation concerned. It is usually manifested in the extent and manner in which the state seeks to control the activities of its citizens.

The **macroeconomic** environment is concerned with the view of the economy as a whole whereas the **microeconomic** perspective was concerned with the individual enterprise. Since one is made up of the other, they both interact and affect each other, but each has a distinctive point of view. In macroeconomics we are concerned with **aggregate variables** such as the total demand and total supply rather than those of the individual firm. However, in common with microeconomics, we are concerned with the **relationships** between each of these aggregate variables and the effect they have on the overall level of economic activity, which is now the main focus of attention.

2.0 Key Points

The purpose of this chapter will be;

- to construct a simple model of the economy - the circular flow of income - and identify key economic variables;
- to note the difference in emphasis in explanation of the operation of the economy offered by Classical, Keynesian and Monetarist economists;
- to examine the bases on which the material wealth of an economy is measured;
- note the main policy objectives adopted by U.K. governments;
- identify the economic variables which are crucial to the fulfillment of these objectives;

- examine how these variables can be affected by monetary and fiscal policy;
- examine the techniques or "tools" of monetary and fiscal policy in some detail.

3.0 The Economic System

Our analysis of the macroeconomic environment begins with a simple model of the economy. It identifies the two main types of "flows" in the economy already identified in chapter 2, namely **real** flows and **money** flows. These flows can be represented in the simple model illustrated below in figure 4/1.

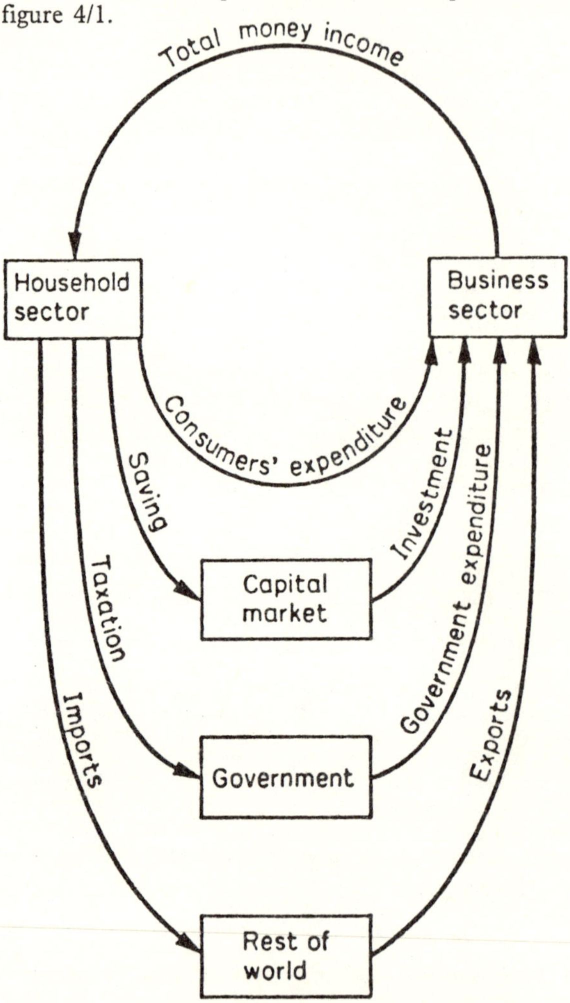

Simple circular flow of income between sectors

Fig. 4/1

3.1 The Circular Flow of Income

The real flows are those of labour, goods and services, and the money flows are wages, expenditure etc. The simple model assumes in the first instance that there are only two main economic groupings - businesses (the producers) and households (consumers). The flows arise from the business sector employing members of the household sector to produce the goods in return for the payment of wages, and from expenditure by households on the goods and services produced by businesses.

Provided no saving or borrowing takes place and supply is always equated with demand, then there will always be a balance between supply and demand. This however is only guaranteed in a **barter economy** where every purchase must be matched by an equal and opposite sale. Only under these conditions will Say's law - that supply creates its own demand - hold true and equilibrium be established. However, if money is introduced to the economy it acts as a **medium of exchange** acceptable to both buyers and sellers in the place of goods and means that consumers no longer have to supply goods acceptable to the other party, (as was the case with barter) but merely require to exchange money for the good desired.

Money however may be held for reasons other than its spending power; the equality of supply and demand can therefore no longer be guaranteed since people may decide not to spend all their income or perhaps to spend more than they have - i.e. borrow against future income.

Since money is also a **store of value** the household may decide not to spend all its income on the goods produced. The result is a reduction in demand which firms may be able to tolerate for a little while but eventually will have to cut production to meet the fall in demand. The demand for factor services will then fall as will total income paid to the factors of production. If households continue to save the same amount of each unit of income earned the process would continue until the effect of the change has worked through the economy resulting in a lower overall level of income and economic activity. The eventual effect on levels of employment will depend on the extent to which factors are willing to accept reduced rewards for their services.

This analysis assumes that all production is for current consumption, which as we mentioned in chapter 2 need not be the case, as some productive output will be directed to the supply of capital goods. Total income of the household sector will therefore be derived from both these sources. If for the moment we assume that the expenditure on capital or investment goods is equivalent to the amount of income saved, the firms producing goods for current consumption will be enabled to maintain production at current levels because the savings from the household sector are being utilised by the investment goods firms. Thus although income is not fully spent on consumption goods, the deficit in aggregate demand is balanced by the demand for investment goods. This is illustrated in the following example:

Example 4/1

Total income p.a.	£300bn

Households save 20% of additional income (Marginal propensity to save (MPS) = 20%)

Hence:

Expenditure	£240bn
Saving	£ 60bn

Total output p.a. is £300bn because £240bn is produced to meet the demands of consumers, the balance being made for producers as capital equipment. The producers of investment goods pay households for their services as factors of production raising total income to £300bn.

This means that all income is continuing to be used and the real and money flows are in balance. There is however no guarantee that if the savings ratio increased to 25% that the demand for investment goods would balance the increased level of savings because the expenditure and investment decisions are taken by two entirely unrelated groups of people. It is likely in fact, that the reduction in the demand for consumption goods may also lead to a reduction in the demand for investment goods, as the suppliers of consumption goods react to the fall in demand for their products.

3.1.2 Determination of the level of income

From our circular flow analysis so far we can see that output (O) and income (Y) are equal in the first instance. Also, that output is made up of consumption (C) and investment (I) goods, income being made up of expenditure on consumption goods (C) and savings (S). By definition therefore, since

$$O = Y$$

then

$$I = S$$

We shall return to this result in a moment.

The circular flow model can be completed by the inclusion of government and external trade sectors.

Government is active in the economy in a variety of ways;

- the provision of goods and services;
- as a consumer of goods and services provided by private enterprises;
- as a redistributor of income, in the form of pensions, family allowance, invalidity benefit etc. These are referred to as **transfer payments** and are distinguished form other activities in that they are a *redistribution* rather than a creation of income.

This expenditure is financed from taxation either directly as income and profit taxes or indirectly as expenditure taxes. An excess of expenditure over income effectively transfers spending power away from government to households, while an excess of taxation revenue over expenditure transfers income from households to government. Government through public expenditure and taxation can therefore play a significant role in the modern economy. We shall return to this later in the chapter.

Thus we can now say that

$$Y = C + I + G$$

and

$$C = Y - T - S$$

where G is government expenditure
T is taxation

so that

$$I + G + (Y - T - S) = Y$$

or

$$I + G = T + S$$

which confirms our earlier contention about the importance of the role of government to the level of economic activity.

If the *net* position of government (T − G) is described as government saving (S_G) - which can be negative or positive - then the concept of the equality between savings and investment can be preserved and the importance of the government contribution highlighted.

As can be appreciated, the external trade of a nation will have an effect on the circular flow. Foreign trade leads to further real and money flows. Exports (X) are not consumed in their country of origin, but earn revenue for the factors involved in their production. They constitute an addition to the circular flow. Imports (M) on the other hand are a leakage from the circular flow because domestic factor incomes spent on foreign produced goods create income for overseas producers. The final effect on the circular flow depends on the balance of trade between the domestic economy and the rest of the world. Thus if $X > M$, the circular flow will be increased, whereas $X < M$ will have the opposite effect.

To summarise:

Total output can be expressed as:

$$C + I + G + X$$

or

$$Y + M.$$

Since

$$C = Y - T - S$$

then

$$Y - T - S + I + G + X = Y + M$$

and

$$I + G + X = M + T + S$$

We have already seen that $T - G = S_G$

likewise

$$X - M = I_O$$

where I_O is overseas investment.

Hence the equality between savings and investment is further preserved as summarised below:

$$I_O + I = S + S_G$$

This equality between saving and investment is important as we will see in the next section. For the present it is sufficient to note that if the level of investment, or injections, to the circular flow is greater than the level of savings, income levels and economic activity will increase. If the opposite is the case then the circular flow will be reduced and economic activity, income and investment levels will fall.

3.2 The Adjustment Process

From one point of view the circular flow will always balance, and investment and saving will always be equal. This is known as the *ex post* (actual or realized) position. This is the after-the-event perspective, and since the circular flow is a money flow this means that these variables will always be in balance. This however is not particularly helpful to an understanding of the operation of the economy. What would be more interesting would be to observe how the economy reaches this position of balance if it has been in imbalance. Of much interest to economists are the variables which are crucial to the process of adjustment, because an understanding of these and how they interact with the others yields powerful policy tools for management of the economy.

The analysis therefore proceeds from an *ex ante* position, i.e. planned or intended values of savings or investment. It is unlikely that these will be equal because investment and savings decisions are taken by widely varying groups of people whose plans and objectives will be unrelated.

According to the **Classical** economists these varying intentions are reconciled by means of **the rate of interest** at a point where total supply and total demand would be in equilibrium. This conclusion is based on assumptions made by the Classical economists regarding conditions in the factor markets. The outcome of these assumptions was that the economy would always tend towards a position of full employment equilibrium — that is, the 'natural' point of balance of the economy would be in conditions of full employment. Given this supposed tendency of the system to automatically correct imbalances, the main policy implication was that of minimum government interference in economic affairs.

This account of the process of adjustment was rejected by **J.M. Keynes** as inadequate in the light of economic experience during the 1920s and 30s. His ideas became particularly influential in post-war economic policy making, being eclipsed only in the latter years of the 1970s by monetarist policy. Keynes argued that the necessary adjustment to bring savings equal to investment took place in the **level of income** or economic activity. His conclusion was that equilibrium could occur even if there were unemployed resources - a conclusion borne out by the facts of the time.

Keynes argued that the level of business expectations and the proportion of each pound earned by factors that was re-spent (the **marginal**

propensity to consume) were important determinants of the overall level of income or economic activity. The following example illustrates the role of the level of income in the restoration of the equilibrium position.

Example 4/2

National income (Y) £250bn
MPC 0.68

therefore: C = 0.68(£250)bn
= £170bn
S = £ 80bn
I = £ 80bn

Since businessmen are confident about the coming year they are prepared to increase the amount of goods and services provided by 10%, which will require a similar increase in the amount of capital equipment ordered.

Thus ex ante I = +10%
but ex ante S = + 0%

From these projections the total level of savings would appear to be £8bn short of that required to support the additional investment. This difference will be made up as a result of the increase in income arising from the increased level of investment.

The net addition to the previous year's income of £250bn as a result of these plans is £8bn. The ultimate effect of this injection of funds depends on the marginal propensity to consume (MPC), which in turn affects the value of the **multiplier.**

3.2.1 The multiplier

A proportion of every additional pound added to the circular flow of income is re-spent by the recipient of the original injection. For example if a company decides to build a new factory or increase the existing workforce the additional wages that are paid to those recruited to construct the factory or increase production will in turn be spent in the local community on housing, food, clothing etc. This in turn will be spent by the shopkeepers and companies providing these services so that for every extra pound of investment there will be more than one additional pound of expenditure. The proportion of each additional pound that is added to the circular flow that is then spent is as we have seen the marginal propensity to consume. This fraction determines the overall effect of any additional investment on the circular flow.

The multiplier (k) is the reciprocal of the marginal propensity to save which itself is calculated as 1 − MPC. Since an MPC of 0.68 infers a value of k of 3.125, the total increase in income is

£8bn × 3.125 = £25bn

which means that
Y = £275bn
C = £187bn
S = £ 88bn
I = £ 88bn

The level of saving has now increased to meet the original increase in the level of investment, the adjustment taking place through the increase in the level of income as predicted above.

This example has ignored, for the sake of clarity, treatment of taxation and imports. As we have already noted these are also a leakage from the circular flow and have a similar effect to savings. The main practical effect of their inclusion in the example would be to reduce the value of the multiplier by reducing the MPC. After allowing for such additional leakages and other complicating factors, the current value of the U.K. multiplier is estimated to be approximately 1.5.

3.2.2 The Accelerator

In the example we have just examined we noted that the decisions of businessmen would be affected by their expectations regarding the level of demand for their products. This relationship between the level of investment and the level of income is known as the **acceleration principle.**

The principle states that the level of investment is dependent on the rate of change in demand, which implies that investment may be falling even if there is still an absolute increase in the level of effective demand. The demand for investment goods is therefore more volatile than the demand for consumption goods.

Interaction between the multiplier and accelerator is used to account for the cyclical pattern of economic activity often referred to as "booms" and "slumps". An increase in the level of demand - as measured in terms of consumption expenditure - is reflected in increased sales of consumer products and ultimately the demand for investment, or capital, goods. The demand for capital goods has two components: i) replacement of worn or obsolete equipment; and ii) additions to the stock of capital goods - *new* investment. Increased demand for capital goods will affect the latter of these categories. Not only is the capital stock increased as a result of this change, it also implies that the demand for replacement capital will eventually increase. The increased demand for capital goods will lead to another round of increases in total output as the volume of capital goods grows which will fuel further expenditure on consumer goods and create even higher demand for capital goods. The accelerator and multiplier will "feed off" each other and will continue to reinforce each other until the "circle" is broken by a reduction in the rate of consumption expenditure.

The change will be felt most keenly in the capital goods industries as no expansion is now required to meet demand. The now higher level of stock will be sufficient to meet the new level of demand so that only replacement investment is required. As the output of capital goods falls this will be reflected in a lower demand for factor services and hence a reduction in the level of income. The multiplier will now start to operate in the opposite direction and a contraction will set in until there is a new stimulus in demand and the whole cycle begins again.

Different industries display different cyclical patterns; for example, the fluctuations in the capital goods industries lag behind those in GDP. The identification of these trends are of particular value to the firm if it is to be able to relate its activities to the wider context of the economy. Such knowledge is necessary for the formulation of effective business planning.

4.0 National Income Accounts

Discussions on the theoretical aspects of the economic system presume the ability to measure the variables under examination. National income statistics provide the raw material for the analysis and interpretation of actual economic situations. Since the total output of any economy comprises a wide range of goods and services which can be measured in many different ways - volume, weight, length etc., national income is measured in monetary units. This basis is employed, despite its inadequacies, as it is the only common unit of measurement of the vast range of a nation's output.

In section 3, we saw that output could be measured in terms of total income earned, total production or total expenditure. The practical measurement of national income statistics is carried out on each of these bases. Since we are dealing with the economy as a whole, the results from each method of measurement should be identical as the circular flow model infers that expenditure on production becomes the income of households which in turn becomes further expenditure and so on.

4.1 National Income

This is calculated by summing the total income of all residents of the country in question, plus the difference between the income received from abroad by residents and income paid to non-residents for the supply of goods and services. These payments represent the rewards paid to the factors of production and are referred to as factor incomes. As this total refers to current consumption only it is adjusted to allow for the amount of fixed resources used up in the production in any one year - capital consumption. This is also referred to as deprcciation and indicates the amount of reinvestment that would be required to maintain the same level of capital resources.

Transfer payments are not included in the total because they are redistributions of income being paid from factor incomes through taxes or national insurance schemes.

4.2 National Product

The value of domestic production is calculated by summing the values added during each stage of production. The value added method is used to avoid the problem of double-counting because each product sold in the market place has been through many different stages in the production process. The correct measurement of value for each stage of production is the contribution to the value of the product that it has made. The market price of each item sold in the market will in fact be the sum of the values added for that product.

Output can be valued at either market price or factor cost. The difference is that market price includes any indirect taxes or subsidies and is the price paid in the market. The difference in value between market price and factor cost will be paid to the government in the form of taxes.

The total value of domestically produced goods, valued according to either basis, is known as the **gross domestic product** (GDP). Adding net income from abroad gives the total output and return on all investment by residents of the country, whether at home or abroad, and is referred to as the **gross national product.** Deducting a figure for capital consumption gives **net national product,** or national income as it is more commonly known. In theory this figure will be identical to that calculated on the basis of factors incomes, although the practicalities of constructing national income statistics usually means that a balancing item - "residual error" - has to be incorporated to bring about equality.

4.3 National Expenditure

Domestic expenditure is the value of residents' expenditure on consumption and investment goods, including their import content. It is calculated by summing all final expenditures, thus eliminating the problem of double-counting by excluding the intermediate expenditures involved in bringing a product to its final stages of completion. Therefore on ly figures for sales plus any items added to holdings of stocks are included in the figure.

Since total final expenditure includes that arising from foreign trade it is calculated by adding the net position on foreign trade (exports minus imports) to domestic expenditure.

5.0 Economic policy

The various analyses by economic theorists have led to the adoption of differing policy measures by governments to achieve declared economic policy objectives. It should be noted that governments now accept responsibility for economic management as an inevitable function of government. As the volume of research and analysis has increased so too have the range of "tools" of economic management. In many countries the difference between the political parties seeking power is differences of emphasis within a range of policy alternatives, rather than the objectives pursued.

5.1 Economic Policy Objectives

Government in the U.K. has a number of specific economic objectives:

1. the achievement and maintenance of a full employment level of economic activity;
2. a continuous and reasonably steady rate of economic growth as measured by year on year changes in the level of GDP;
3. stability in the general level of prices. Normally measured by the retail prices index.
4. the maintenance of a balance on external trade.

These objectives are normally concerned with macroeconomic activity. In addition government has a number of microeconomic policy objectives concerning regional development and competition.

A balance has to be maintained between the different policy objectives. For example the achievement "full" employment (which is never actually possible as a result of people moving between jobs, people unable to work and those not offering themselves for paid employment such as housewives), may only be possible at the expense of one of the other policy objectives.

High employment and steady growth which are conducive to the stimulation of further investment, innovation and increased productivity, may lead to a situation where the level of demand outstrips the ability of the economy to produce sufficient goods to meet the demand. This excess demand would also be seen in the factor markets. The result would be an increase in the general level of prices (inflation), thereby frustrating the goal of price stability.

Price inflation in turn has a further range of effects:

- alteration in the relative prices of the factors of production will eventually result in an alteration of production methods;
- it may lead to changes in the levels of production;
- complication of the task of investment appraisal;
- redistribution of income away from those on fixed incomes in favour of those on incomes related to the level of prices. Salesmen on commission and companies earning profits are in a better position to weather inflation than are students or pensioners on fixed incomes.
- reduction in international competitiveness as domestically produced goods become relatively more expensive in world markets. The inevitable result is a balance of payments deficit which eventually gives rise to pressure on the value of the currency of the country in question i.e. its purchasing power is reduced.

As indicated therefore, government is often faced with conflicting objectives. The final decision is a political rather than an economic one.

5.2 Relevant Economic Variables

In our previous analysis we saw that certain economic variables were of importance for the overall level of economic activity. Namely:

- the level of expenditure;
- the level of saving;
- the level of investment;
- the level of interest rates;
- the balance on foreign trade;
- the extent of government involvement; and
- the rate of change in the money supply.

In particular, (i) the level of planned expenditure; (ii) the absolute level of costs; and (iii) relativities between domestic and international price levels (exchange rates) are important to governments seeking to achieve their stated objectives by the manipulation of economic variables.

Therefore if the problem is one of unemployment, deflation and balance of payments deficits, then appropriate action would be to increased the level of spending and alter the exchange rate to alter the prices of domestic goods in world markets and produce balance of payments balance. Unfortunately, neither the problems or their solution are as easily identified or implemented as this. The above scenario implicitly assumed that any increase in the level of prices would be due solely to excess demand. Price inflation may also be the result of changes in the cost of factors - changes over which even a government may have little control. The resulting impact on the system may however be severe, as in the oil crises of the 1970s.

5.3 Economic Policy Instruments

Governments seek to control these variables by means of **monetary** and **fiscal** policy instruments. Monetary policy instruments are chiefly concerned with the supply and cost of money. Fiscal policy instruments such as government expenditure and taxation are used to influence the level of economic activity by increasing or reducing the circular flow. Both sets of tools are available to governments.

The main impact of Keynesian theory was its advocacy of the active role of government in the economy. Keynes demonstrated that insufficient demand would not automatically be rectified by market forces, as the slack in consumption demand would not be balanced by the demand for investment goods, since this demand was derived from the demand for consumption goods. This shortfall led to equilibrium with unemployed resources. As Keynes had dismissed the rate of interest and the money supply as variables that could have a significant effect on economic activity, greater emphasis was placed on the role which government could play in stimulating the economy through the judicious use of fiscal policy instruments such as expenditure and taxation.

Much of the work of the Monetarist economists has been directed at re-establishing the rate of interest and the supply of money as important determinants of economic activity. Their arguments have gained favour as Keynesian fiscal policies failed to control the inflationary surge of the 1970s.

Monetarism is a longer term approach than that of Keynesianism. Its principal recommendation is that the rate of growth in the supply of money must be tailored to the rate of growth of the economy, otherwise inflation will result. From the point of view of the business the main impact has been the change in emphasis in economic policy towards the monetary policy instruments of money supply and the rate of interest.

6.0 Monetary Policy

Monetary policy is concerned with controlling the level of demand through controlling the supply and cost of money. Money however is not simply the quantity of notes and coin in circulation, but is a wider concept. Different measures of money are required because of the various functions that money performs, namely

— as a **a medium of exchange,** for use in the purchase of goods and services;

— as **a store of value** for savings;

— as **a standard for deferred payments** for use in credit transactions;

— as **a unit of value** for pricing.

The measures of money stock in the U.K. are known as M0, M1, M2, sterling M3 (£M3), M3c, M4 and M5. The component parts of each of these measures, with the exception of M0, are identified in table 4/1.

M0, referred to as the wide monetary base, comprises the amount of notes and coin in circulation with the public plus operational deposits held by the clearing banks with the Bank of England. M0 is also known as 'narrow money' and is one of the main indicators of the level and rate of growth of money stock in the U.K.

Another important indicator is M4, usually referred to as the broad measure of money. From table 4/1 it can be seen that the components of M4 are:

— interest and non-interest bearing sterling sight deposits of the private sector (largely current or cheque accounts); plus

— sterling time bank deposits; plus

— private sector sterling bank certificates of deposit (CDs); plus

— private sector holdings of building society shares, deposits and CDs net of any building society holdings of bank deposits, bank CDs and notes and coin.

6.1 Monetary Policy Instruments

Government control over the banking system is exercised through the medium of the Bank of England in the following ways:

6.1.1 Moral suasion

As a result of its particularly close relationship with the commercial banking system and certain powers conferred on it at the time of its nationalisation (1946), the Bank is able to exert an influence on the behaviour of banks in the U.K. without resort to legislation or ministerial authority.

6.1.2 Reserve requirements

Despite the ability of the banking system overall to increase the amount of credit individual banks require, in the interests of financial prudence, to retain a certain proportion of all deposits made with them in liquid form. Government can influence the banks ability to lend by insisting that a minimum ratio of assets to liabilities be held in a readily realisable form therefore restricting the volume of lending.

6.1.3 Open market operations

This refers to Government activity in the capital and money markets. Any shortfall in government revenue over expenditure has to be met by borrowing. This is financed by selling government loan stock in the form of Gilt-edged stock in the long term market or Treasury Bills in the short-term market. Gilts are issued at maturities ranging from 5 to 30 years, and Bills for 91 days. Government can therefore operate in the Stock or Treasury Bill markets to accommodate its needs.

These funding operations can also be used as a means of control of the money supply. As non-bank institutions prevail in the stock markets, selling government debt to these holders effectively reduces the banks' collective ability to create credit because the cheques which are drawn to buy the gilts reduce the deposits held by the banks. This policy of soaking up excess credit by means of gilt sales to the public is known as **overfunding.**

Since this policy requires the sale of large amounts of government loan stock, a sufficiently attractive return has to be offered in order to guarantee a successful issue, thus affecting the level of interest rates throughout the economy.

The Treasury bill market is occupied principally by the clearing banks, discount houses - a small group of specialist financial intermediaries - and the Bank of England. Its chief function is the financing of short-term government debt and thereby the level of interest rates. The current arrangements are that the Bank will on a daily basis be prepared to purchase Bills within a band of undisclosed rates which can be calculated by the market from details of its operation in the market released later in the day.

The aim of these operations is to control the demand for money by controlling its cost to the "consumer", and forms the mainstay of monetary control measures at the time of writing.

6.1.4 The discount rate.

The Bank of England, the clearing banks and the discount houses participate in the discount market which is the "official" U.K. money market. Similar markets exist in other economies. This market provides the banking system with a pool of liquidity to rectify overnight shortages in cash balances or a means of deposit for overnight funds. It performs a "smoothing" operation whereby banks with excess balances lend those funds to banks with shortages through the medium of the discount houses who are the market makers. The Bank of England is only involved when the net position in the market is that of shortage. The Bank will then lend to the discount houses in its capacity as **lender of last resort** by purchasing Treasury Bills or by granting a direct loan . The rate at which it lends - the discount rate - has variously been known as Bank Rate or Minimum Lending Rate (M.L.R.). The significance of this rate is that it determines the cost of borrowing for the entire economy.

6.2 Target Variables

The various strands of monetary policy are coordinated and their effectiveness measured by reference to selected "target variables". The target variables are set as the indicators of the successful execution of monetary policies. The provisions of the current medium term financial strategy (MTFS) have been set with the overall objective of controlling inflation. The variables crucial to that success have been identified and acceptable levels specified which are consistent with the overall goal. Thus the policy of the MTFS is to control inflation by means of

i) the balance between government expenditure and revenues. This is referred to as either the Public Sector Borrowing Requirement (PSBR) where expenditure exceeds income, or the Public Sector Debt Repayment (PSDR) when the opposite is the case;

and

ii) the level of bank lending, as measured by the range of monetary aggregates mentioned above.

The target variables are therefore

1. the level of PSBR or PSDR — in terms of a percentage of Gross Domestic Product. For example this is planned to be 1.75% for 1990/1.
2. the annual rate of growth of M0 - measured in percentage terms and usually expressed as a range of values within which the rate is expected to fall: with effect from March 1987 this indicator has been adopted as the sole measure of the money stock within the terms of the MTFS;
3. the annual rate of growth of M4 - as with M0 this has in the past been expressed in terms of a band of values. Although this is no longer officially a target variable within the MFTS it level will continue to be monitored by government, as will the other variables described in table 4/1 overleaf.

If the actual is less than the target in instance, the implication is that the policy objective is being achieved.

7.0 Fiscal Policy

Fiscal policy is the use of government expenditure and taxation as means of influencing the level of economic activity. Their use in this connection is closely linked to Keynesian economic policies. Although monetary policies are currently favoured as the most effective means of controlling economic activity, tools of fiscal continue to be used as part of overall economic strategy.

Relationships among the monetary and liquidity aggregates and their components

Notes and coin in circulation with the public

plus Banks' till money

plus Banks' operational balances with the Bank of England

equals **Wide monetary base, MO**

plus Private sector non-interest-bearing sterling sight bank deposits

equals **Non-interest-bearing component of M_1**

plus Private sector interest-bearing retail sterling bank deposits

plus Private sector holdings of retail building society deposits and national savings bank ordinary accounts

equals **M_2**

plus Private sector interest-bearing sterling sight bank deposits

equals **M_1**

plus Private sector sterling time bank deposits —original maturity of up to two years

plus Private sector holdings of sterling bank certificates of deposit

plus Private sector holdings of money-market instruments (bank bills, Treasury bills, local authority deposits) and certificates of tax deposit

equals **PSL_1**

plus Private sector holdings of building society deposits (excluding term shares and SAYE) and national savings instruments (excluding certificates, SAYE and other longer-term deposits)

less Building society holdings of money-market instruments and bank deposits etc

equals **PSL_2**

plus Private sector sterling time bank deposits —original maturity of over two years

equals **Sterling M_3**

plus Private sector foreign currency bank deposits

equals **Total M_3**

Table 4/1

7.1 Government Expenditure

This takes the form of **capital projects** such as investment in the social infrastructure - roads, electrification of railways, school buildings - and also nationalised industries; **current expenditure** such as civil and public servants salaries, rate support grant, social security payments and other benefits; and subsidies, grants and allowances.

Government expenditure is undertaken to inject additional income to the circular flow, which in accordance with the multiplier theory, should yield a greater return than the initial injection. According to Keynesian theory, these injections of public funds were necessary to supplement consumption and investment expenditure when the level of economic activity was at less than full employment.

7.2 Revenue

Government also generates revenue through the trading surpluses (profits) of nationalised industries, the proceeds from the transfer of these industries to public ownership (privatisation) and taxation.

7.2.1 Taxation

Taxation is the single largest source of government revenue. It is also an extremely important tool of economic management.

The main forms of taxation are classified as to whether they are:

- **direct taxation,** where the cost is borne directly by the person on whom it is levied, for example income tax, corporation tax, development land tax, rates, road fund license, petroleum land tax etc.; or
- **indirect taxation,** where the cost, or at least part of the cost can be passed on either as a fixed amount such as in many customs duties or as a percentage as in the case of VAT.

The switch in emphasis from direct to indirect taxation which was introduced in 1979 continues to the time of writing.

In figure 4/1 taxation was identified as a withdrawal from the circular flow of income. Government is therefore able to reduce the level of households' expenditure by increasing the level of taxation. This can be used to reduce inflationary pressures by reducing the overall level of consumer demand. It should be noted that the multiplier effect also comes into operation in this connection producing a greater overall reduction than the original amount withdrawn from the circular flow. Alternatively a reduction in levels of taxation can be used to stimulate demand by increasing the amount of disposable income, thereby providing a stimulus for the level of economic activity.

7.3 The Budget

Government expenditure and revenue plans are announced in the Budget, which usually contains an interesting precis of the official view of the state of the economy. The budget is the major legislative tool of economic management as its proposals are incorporated in the Finance Act.

It is usual for the incumbent Chancellor to outline the economic policies which the government intend to pursue in the Budget, giving details of monetary targets, planned levels of expenditure, rates of taxation etc. It also reports on the excess of expenditure over revenue and therefore the extent to which the government has to borrow to fund the difference. The shortfall is referred to as the Central Government Borrowing Requirement, which together with a similar requirement for local authorities and public corporation constitute the P.S.B.R. The importance of this as an influence on the rate of growth of the money supply and the consequent results for inflation has already been discussed. The sum of successive PSBRs, or budget deficits is the National Debt, management for which is the responsibility of the Bank of England. The methods of funding government borrowing requirement - Treasury bills and gilt-edged stock have already been discussed under monetary policy.

8.0 Microeconomic Policy

This area of policy concern deals with the areas of regional development and competition.

8.1 Regional Policy

This deals with the issues of unequal regional development and associated problems of unemployment, deprivation and urban decay.

An outstanding feature of regional policy is the bewildering array of incentives, special schemes, grants, subsidies, etc that are available from both the U.K. government and the E.E.C; and the regional variations in the help that is available.

8.2 Competition Policy

The aim of the policy initiatives in this area is encouragement in the level of competition in the market place this being perceived as the principal means of stimulating more efficient allocation of resources thus leading to more competitively priced goods on world markets, to greater demand for U.K. goods resulting eventually in increased employment.

Much of the provision in this area is in the form of legislation, either seeking to prevent or control the concentration of economic power. The principal tools of control are:

- the Monopolies and Mergers Commission;
- the Office of the Director General of Fair Trading;

- the Restrictive Practices Act 1956;
- the Consumer Protection Advisory Committee;
- the Consumer Credit Act 1974.

9.0 Summary

In this chapter we have presented a circular flow model of the operation of the economy and how this theoretical base forms the means by which the "income" of a country is measured in the national income accounts.

Although it cannot hope to replicate the complexities of a modern mixed economy, the circular flow model has allowed us to identify economic variables which hold the key to the level of economic activity, namely: the levels of expenditure, saving, investment and interest rates, the balance on foreign trade, and the rate of change in the money supply.

We also noted the disagreement between Classical, Keynesian and Monetarist economists as to which variables have the greatest influence on the level of economic activity and the difference in economic policy to which such analyses have given rise.

Monetary policy, it was noted, operated principally by seeking to control demand through control of the cost of borrowing, whereas the aim of fiscal policy was to control the level of economic activity through the balance between government revenue and expenditure.

The range of U.K. policy objectives at both micro and macro level was cited as an example of the kind of targets which governments set themselves in the field of economic management - objectives which may often not be possible to achieve simultaneously, thus requiring a measure of reconciliation between conflicting objectives.

10.0 Conclusions

The pursuit by government of the economic objectives outlined earlier by means of fiscal and monetary tools impact on the activities of the individual enterprise. The fortunes of the individual enterprise are therefore inevitably bound up with the economic health of the nation in which it is located, even although this may not be immediately apparent.

Even the achievement of certain goals such as stable and full employment levels is fragile and fraught with difficulties such as the possibility of a rise in inflationary pressures. Price instability gives rise to the problem of under-insurance, a problem which can be reduced by adjustment of the relevant values by application of an index of prices. The index chosen should however be relevant to the items under consideration. For instance it is unlikely that the Retail Prices Index (RPI) is wholly appropriate to a manufacturing environment.

The effects of monetary and fiscal policy may also be important. The main threats which monetary policy may pose to the enterprise are in relation to its own borrowing and also those of its suppliers. In a period of high levels of real interest rates credit management becomes more important as the risk of default and the cost to the business of financing bad debts is increased accordingly. Higher interest rates are also inimical to investment activity.

Fiscal policies of rapid expansion in government expenditure creates such dangers as inflationary pressure and balance of payment problems. The possibility of under-insurance is increased in such circumstances as is the threat of industrial action as employees seek to recover reductions in living standards through increased wage settlements as the increase in domestic price levels is pushed higher as the result of higher import prices. Alternatively a stricter tax regime may lead to reduced allowances for capital expenditures - including safety and loss reduction equipment, and reduced demand as the level of personal and corporate disposable income is reduced.

For companies with interests in export markets, the economic health of both exporting and importing nations should be of interest. Firstly, exchange rate stability, based on balanced trading performance operates to the benefit of exporters and importers alike as the level of uncertainty and exchange risk is reduced. Secondly, the risk of credit default is reduced. If an exporter is in a position to assess the performance of the importing government's economic management by the identification and analysis of key economic variables such as the level of expenditure, rate of growth in the money supply or level of prices, then it is better able to manage its overseas credit risk.

Chapter Five

THE INTERNATIONAL ECONOMIC ENVIRONMENT — Balance of Payments and Exchange Rates

1.0 International Trade

International trade occurs for a variety of reasons including the distribution of natural resources, climatic variances, population distribution and density, strategic considerations and the gains arising from trade as detailed by the doctrine of comparative advantage.

The doctrine of comparative advantage states that, within limits imposes by their terms of trade, nations should specialise not only in the production of and trade in those commodities in which they have an absolute advantage, but also those in which they have a comparative advantage. A comparative advantage exists when one country is relatively more efficient in the production of a good than another, which creates the opportunity for trade. According to the doctrine if the more efficient nation specialises in the production of this good and leaves production of the other good to the less efficient country, there will be an overall gain for the two countries provided trade is allowed to take place.

The conclusion therefore is that the utilisation of the world's resources can be optimised if peoples specialise in the production of goods in which they have the greatest comparative advantage or the least comparative disadvantage leaving others to produce commodities of which they are inefficient producers. These gains however are only realised if trade between nations is allowed to take place with the minimum of restrictions.

The terms of trade, measured by the volume of goods from the domestic economy that have to be traded to earn the income to buy one unit of imports, which dictate the boundaries within which the benefits from trade can be realised, are themselves determined by the health of the domestic economy, for example the rate of inflation, growth in GNP or level of employment.

The terms of trade measure the amount of imports that a country could purchase with one unit of its exports. In practice the terms of trade are measured by the ratio of export prices to import prices as below:

$$\text{Index terms of trade} = \frac{\text{price index of exports}}{\text{price index of imports}} \times \frac{100}{1}$$

The terms of trade are said to improve if they exceed 100 or deteriorate if they fall below it. They are determined by the relative economic performances of the trading countries in terms of such indicators as inflation, level of employment or rate of economic growth. The importance of the terms of trade is that they set the boundaries between which the benefits of trade can be realised.

The theory therefore advocates the ideal of free trade, and has in practical terms led to such policy initiatives as the General Agreement on Tariffs and Trade (GATT), which is a commitment from the major trading nations of the world to the eventual elimination of all barriers to free trade, and the development of free trade areas such as the European Free Trade Area (EFTA) and customs unions such as the European Economic Community (EEC).

The theoretical benefits of trade are however mitigated by such factors as the absence of equally productive factors in each country, a lack of reciprocal demand, the existence of tariffs and quotas, transport costs and the requirement of most countries to retain certain industries for reasons of strategy.

2.0 Key Points

The purpose of this chapter will be to:

- examine the structure of the balance of payments;
- consider the remedies available to correct an imbalance on the balance of payments, and note the implications for the individual firm;
- explain the meaning and determination of a rate of exchange;
- examine various systems of exchange rate operation;
- note the effect of different systems on the volatility of exchange rate movements and the different mechanisms that exist to reduce exposure to currency risk.

3.0 Balance of Payments

The movement of goods and services across national boundaries creates an equal and opposite flow of money in settlement of the underlying transactions.

3.1 Settlement of Trading Debts

The various means by which foreign trade is undertaken, financed and settled are highly specialised and reference would have to be made to the appropriate sources for further information, but in summary an awareness of:

- the channels of overseas trade, e.g.from export merchants to overseas subsidiaries;
- the relevant contract law;
- the terms of sale; and
- the methods of payment;

would be necessary to appreciate the nature of the additional areas of pure risk raised by foreign trade. It should be noted that some measure of international agreement has been reached in respect of terms of sale and methods of settlement, and are contained in the rules of the International Chamber of Commerce.

3.2 Structure

The balance of payments is a record of the flows of money between nations and a calculation of the position of the home country relative to the rest of the world. Some have suggested the analogy of a profit and loss account as an explanation of the concept of the balance of payments of, for example 'U.K. Ltd'.

A simplification of the structure of the balance of payments would be as follows:

the balance of trade on visible goods
+ the balance of trade on 'invisibles'

the balance on the current account

+ the balance on the capital account

the balance for official financing

This figure is known as the **balance for official financing** or change in official reserves, and implies that strictly speaking the balance of payments will always be in balance as the balance of payments is merely a book-keeping system bounded by the rules of double-entry. The implications however of a continuing deficit - although balanced by borrowing in the first instance - are that as the trend continues the country concerned will find it increasingly difficult to raise the necessary finance on the world money markets. The accompanying decline in its trading and financial position will mean that a country cannot sustain such a movement over a protracted period as a liquidity crisis will eventually result as the country finds itself unable to meet its international debts. The analogy of a company trading at a loss is not difficult to see.

This figure is known as the **balance for official financing,** and implies that strictly speaking the balance of payments will always be in balance as the balance of payments is merely a book-keeping system bounded by the rules of double-entry. The implications however of a continuing deficit - although balanced by borrowing in the first instance - are that as the trend continues the country concerned will find it increasingly difficult to raise the necessary finance on the world money markets. The accompanying decline in its trading and financial position will mean that a country cannot sustain such a movement over a protracted period as a liquidity crisis will eventually result as the country finds itself unable to meet its international debts. The analogy of a company trading at a loss is not difficult to see.

The main consequence of such a situation for the individual company is the corrective action that a government will have to take to remedy the situation.

3.3 Policies

In the case of a deficit, the objective of remedial measures will be the reduction of spending on imports accompanied by an increase in the volume of exports. These goals can be accomplished by changes in either the volume or prices of exports and imports. In summary these will include those directly affecting **volume:**

- **reduction of the volume of imports** by such means as import controls, quotas, deposits and exchange controls;
- **reduction of the demand for imports** through the stimulation of import substituting industries;
- **increase the volume of exports** through government assistance in such areas as market research, documentation, advisory services and finance; and those affecting **price:**

- **changes in the exchange rate to make exports more competitive and imports more expensive.**

The results of a change in the exchange rate are difficult to forecast accurately because of other factors such elasticities of demand for exports and imports.

3.4 Longer-term Disequilibrium

An imbalance in the balance of payments should not be unexpected and need give no cause for concern provided it is balanced out in the longer term. Permanent disequilibrium is however an extremely undesirable state of affairs for the reasons outlined above in section 3.2. The range of options open to a country to deal with such problems have already been outlined in section 3.3 above.

The measures adopted will therefore depend on the seriousness of the problem. Initially countries will seek to finance the deficits from their own resources, but this can only be pursued for a limited period. Under a regime of floating exchange rates the adjustment will take place in this area with the currency depreciating against those of its trading partners. The extent of the fall will depend as much on political as economic factors. It is unlikely that a major industrial nation will be prepared, or even allowed, to pursue such a policy indefinitely. Once this avenue has been exhausted and the deficit problem has not been cured restrictions in a number of different forms on imports may be imposed in an attempt to reduce the imbalance in trade. Monetary and fiscal measures to control the domestic economy may be pursued either concurrently with those above or as a last resort.

As deficits continue to accrue during the period of adjustment these will require to be financed in order for the country to honour its overseas trading committments. This finance will be available from firstly the international money markets, secondly under arrangements from central banks of trading partners and finally from the IMF - usually subject to some conditions.

The danger of protectionism - high tariff barriers, imposition of import quotas and quality controls - to an exporter when dealing with such a country is real. The effect on the exchange rate of continued deficit balances will be a constant downward pressure with the uncertainty that this creates for all currency flows to and from the country.

In the long term government will have to correct - or may be required to correct by their international creditors, such as the IMF - the underlying cause of the imbalance. This will probably require the introduction of stringent policy measures into the domestic economy with resulting changes in both monetary and/or fiscal policies.

4.0 Exchange Rates

As we have already stated goods and services are traded but settlement of the debts created is made in money. This gives rise for the need to convert the currency of one country into that of another and therefore to determine the rate at which currencies should be exchanged. The exchange rate is defined as the rate at which one currency can be exchanged for another. In effect it is the price of one currency expressed in terms of another.

For example the UK exporter of goods to the USA receives payment for the goods supplied in dollars but has to pay for materials, labour and overheads in sterling. If the rate of exchange is $1.5 to £1 this means that £1 sterling buys $1.50 worth of goods or cash ; or that $1 buys 67p worth of UK goods.

Currencies are traded in the foreign exchange markets as exporters and importers seek to meet their currency needs. Theoretically at least, the price of a currency will be determined by the market forces of supply and demand, as illustrated in figure 5/1.

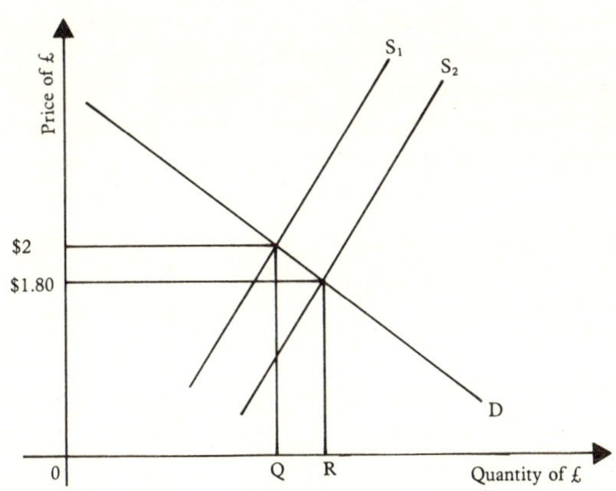

Fig. 5/1

The rate for sterling is expressed in terms of the US dollar, and is dependent upon both the demand for sterling - as the result of UK goods sold in the USA - and its supply - the result of UK spending on goods produced in the USA. The balance between the two establishes the exchange rate. If UK imports of USA goods is greater than than exports then the result will be a reduction in the value of the £ from $2 as the supply of £ has increased. The new equilibrium point is established at $1.80.

Since payment of these funds is normally made by the transfer of funds from one bank account to another, banks are active participants in these markets and 'take a position' in the leading currencies, along with brokers who bring comercial buyers and sellers together. Official participants such as central banks - for example, the Bank of England - and international agencies are also active in the market. The UK foreign exchange market, centred in London, is part of the international market in foreign exchange with trading centres in New York, Singapore, Hong Kong, Tokyo, Zurich, Frankfurt and Paris. The Bank of England participates on behalf of the government, other central banks and international institutions and occasionally to smooth currency fluctuations through the Exchange Equalisation Account.

4.1 Influential Factors

The rate of exchange in the market is determined by a number of factors:

1. **The balance of trade.** If a country has a balance of payments surplus it has sold more than it has bought which means there will be a net demand for its currency in the market with the inevitable consequence for the exchange rate. The position is reversed in the case of a deficit.

2. **Relative prices.** This refers to the respective level of prices or rate of price inflation obtaining in the countries between which trade is taking place. It is based on the theory of purchasing power parity which states that changes in relative price levels will eventually be reflected in the rate of exchange between the two countries. Thus if one country is experiencing a higher rate of inflation than another, the value of its currency in terms of the currency of the other country will decline. Empirical studies of long term movements in exchange rates bear this out.

3. **Level of international interest rates.** A higher rate of interest on deposits in one financial centre e.g. London relative to other centres will attract funds to London and thereby increase the demand for sterling.

4. **Overall economic performance.** Economic variables such as the money supply, industrial relations and productivity are important to economic performance and will therefore influence economic forecasts which will indicate the future need and hence demand for

currency which will then be bought and sold according to the prognosis.

5. **Political factors.** The stability of government, government policy, trade agreements, the possibility and existence of military conflict are only amongst some of the factors which will influence exchange rates. Political risks are discussed at greater length in a later chapter.

6. **Central bank policy.** The central bank normally has responsibility for the management of a country's foreign currency reserves. The extent to which it will be prepared to intervene in the foreign currency markets to either support a currency which is falling by buying it or take pressure off a currency which is rising too fast by selling will also be an influence on the level of currency rates.

4.2 Exchange Rate Systems

The example in figure 5/1 assumed that exchange rates would be allowed to find their own level. It is rare however to find a completely free market.

In the past exchange rates have been tied to the price of gold, firstly directly in the gold standard and the gold exchange standard and then indirectly via the US dollar in the Bretton Woods or IMF system. More recently they have been allowed to 'float' - i.e. find their own level - theoretically without official support. Usually governments which have adopted such a system find it necessary for a variety of reasons to intervene in the manner described earlier, such as in January 1985 when Chancellor Lawson was obliged to take steps to halt the decline of sterling against the dollar. This is referred to as the 'managed' or 'dirty' float. Exchange rate systems can either be fixed to a particular rate (with some allowance made for movements around a 'par' value) or allowed to float.

4.2.3 IMF system

Under this system, which was devised and agreed by the Allies at Bretton Woods in 1944, the value of all currencies would be tied to the US dollar, the value of which was fixed in terms of gold. The result was that the dollar become the mainstay of world liquidity, becoming the universally acceptable means of settling international debts. Under the system a small variation of 1% around the value of the exchange rate that had been fixed for a currency in terms of the dollar (par value) was allowed to accommodate short term imbalances in a country's balance of trade. Countries were expected to ensure that their currency did not move outwith these limits. This was achieved in the short term by selling or buying in support of the currency. Longer term measures included an alteration of domestic policies to correct the reason for the imbalance in trade. If the problems persisted and countries found themselves under strain to maintain the required level, then they were permitted to adjust the par value in the required direction - devalue or revalue as happened in the UK in 1948 and 1967. This however was normally regarded as a measure of last resort.

This system continued until the early 1970s when a number of factors reduced confidence in its ability to fulfill its function. The result was that firstly, the margin of variation was increased to 2.25% and then finally abandoned in favour of a system of floating rates.

The IMF system was not concerned solely with exchange rates but also with the maintenance of international liquidity. Part of these arrangements included the creation of a fund to which all members were expected to contribute and from which they were entitled to 'borrow' or rather, exchange their own currencies for other more internationally acceptable currencies when they were experiencing balance of payments problems. The limit of borrowing was 125% of the subscription to the fund, and was organised in 'tranches' of 25%. To each tranche however were attached increasingly stringent conditions under which funds would be advanced.

4.2.4 Floating rate systems

A number of countries including the UK currently operate in this manner. As we have noted earlier the rates are not necessarily allowed to float completely freely but they are not fixed in any sense to a central value. The benefit to the countries concerned is that to a certain extent domestic policies are insulated from the performance of the country in the world economy.

Under a system of floating exchange rates there theoretically would be no balance of payments problems as the exchange rate would always move to reflect the demand and supply for a country's goods. Thus the exchange rate absorbs the changes that previously would have had to have been made under the IMF regime. If a country's domestic economy is becoming increasingly uncompetitive in relation to the rest of the world, this will be reflected in the exchange rate which will fall. Under the IMF system the result would have been increasingly large deficits on the balance of payments.

The operation of floating rates in the real as opposed to theoretical world is hindered in a number of ways, with the result that surpluses and deficits are still recorded on the balance of trade.

We have also noted that exchange rates are affected by more than the single variable of the balance of trade discussed above.

Another feature of the collapse of the IMF system of fixed rates was the decline of the importance of the dollar as a form of international liquidity. A multiple currency reserve has since been adopted so that the Deutschmark, Swiss franc, French franc, Yen, Sterling and Guilder have become acceptable as means of settling international indebtedness. International liquidity is also supplemented by SDRs (Special Drawing Rights) issued by the IMF, which are valued by reference to a weighted basket of currencies.

4.2.5 European Monetary System

Following the collapse of the IMF arrangements the members of the E.E.C. (with the exception of the UK) as part of their overall goal of full monetary union entered into the EMS in 1979, the principal aim of which is exchange rate stability.

The system is based on the ECU (European Currency Unit) which is calculated by reference to a formula which is based on the fixed amount of each members' currency weighted according to its importance in the community as measured in terms of Gross Domestic Product. The ECU is central to the operation of the system as it acts as

a) the denominator for the exchange rate mechanism;

b) the basis for the divergence indicator;

c) the denominator for operations in the intervention and credit mechanism; and

d) a means of settlement between the monetary authorities of the community.

The system operates in the following manner:

- each currency is expressed in terms of ECUs, this is known as the **central rate**;
- variations of up to 2.25% (6% for Italy) either side of this central rate are allowed without any action being required by the country concerned, this is known as the **threshold of divergence.** Once this is threatened the country is required to take corrective action.

In addition to the exchange rate system the EMS is also concerned with the provision of credit support, whereby countries can borrow from 3 months to 5 years depending on the nature of the problem to support their currency.

5.0 Risk Management Perspectives

From the point of view of the risk manager overseas trade not only increases the scale of the problems already faced in the domestic economy, such as distribution, transport and safety but also adds a number of new areas of risk.

Movements in exchange rates can adversely affect revenue and costs as the revenue generated by exports and costs incurred in the importation of raw materials are both affected by exchange rate movements. A movement in the exchange rate which makes exports cheaper, and hopefully more competitive, also makes imports more expensive. If sales do not respond to the reduction in price on the world markets then profit margins will be squeezed.

If a company is seeking to reduce insurance costs through a programme of self-funding of a range of loss costs it must be alert to the additional risks imposed if some of the exposures covered by the fund are situation outwith the country in which the fund is located. As losses will probably have to be paid in the local currency then exchange risks will be incurred. Similar considerations apply for contributions to the fund received from subsidiaries, plants etc located overseas.

Floating rate exchange systems generally increase the levels of uncertainty which will have important consequences for cash flow as has been discussed above, and also for appraisal of investment projects.

These problems can be mitigated by the use of forward or futures markets. A forward contract allows the purchaser or vendor of currency to fix a rate at which the currency will be bought or sold in advance of the date of the receipt or delivery of the currency. The rate is usually based on the rate prevailing on the date upon which the agreement is made, with adjustments to take account of the period over which the contract is being purchased - e.g. 1 month forward or 6 months forward.

A futures contract is the option to buy/sell currency at a certain rate on a future date. The main difference between forward and futures contracts is that since the futures contract is only an option, it can be abandoned at little cost or perhaps more importantly it can be sold to another party. This possibility of sale creates a market in futures which can be used by both buyers and sellers of currency.

The rates for forward and futures contracts are published daily in the Financial Times and also the financial section of the 'quality' dailies.

Movements in exchange rates are the result of changes in other factors as we have seen earlier in the chapter. Steps taken to correct an imbalance in the balance of trade such as the imposition of quotas and other trade restrictions, controls on the amount of foreign exchange that can be exported from the country and the solutions for problems in the domestic economy will impact on the activity of the business enterprise.

In conclusion we have seen in this chapter the interrelationships between the balance of payments, the rate of exchange and the performance of the domestic economy. None can be isolated from any of the others. The greatest danger therefore would be to compartmentalise each of these areas, as failure to appreciate the consequences of actions taken in one sector reduces the effectiveness of the process of risk identification.

Chapter Six

THE LEGAL ENVIRONMENT — The Sources and Administration of English Law

1.0 Introduction

The busıness enterprise has to conduct its activities within the general framework of the laws adopted by the society (or societies) of which it is a member. Some of these laws are designed specifically to control the behaviour of businesses to the extent that 'business people today face an extensive range of legal restrictions on their activities, and a climate of business law much less favourable to them than at any time in the past'. Compliance with other laws, applicable to the rest of the population in general, arises simply out its duty as a member of society.

The nature, range and extent of laws within any one nation is vast and complex. The business organization is however particularly influenced by the body of law which seeks to regulate the creation of agreements between parties in a business arrangement - i.e. the law of contract. The importance of this body of law is that it regulates the basis of all business activities, and whether this involves suppliers, customers, employees or shareholders the rights and duties of each of the parties are usually determined by the terms and conditions of the contract. Furthermore provision also exists in law to allow an aggrieved party to a contract to seek redress for a breach of the contractual agreement.

Another area with which business has to be concerned is the law of tort, which permits a person to seek redress for harm suffered as the result of the actions of another. Product, public and employer's liability are examples of this area of law.

Laws created by Parliament also affect the activities of the business enterprise in a wide number of areas. From employment legislation to provisions surrounding the sale of goods to responsibility for the health and safety of the workforce, organisations are expected to comply with these statutory arrangements.

This and the following 2 chapters will deal with these topics. Chapter 6 is devoted to an examination of the different areas, sources and procedures of English Law. Chapter 7 deals with contract and chapter 8 concentrates on the law of tort. Throughout the discussion reference will be made to the statutory provisions governing the area under examination.

The risks with which the business organization is confronted in the legal environment are principally the penalties for non-compliance of statutory requirements, actions arising from a breach of contractual agreement and liabilities for harm caused to customers, employees etc. The law however is a two-edged sword in that as well as a source of pure risk it can be employed as part of the risk management strategy of the firm.

2.0 Key Points

The purpose of this chapter is to:

- note the principal divisions that are employed in the classification of the vast body of law;
- examine briefly the major sources of English law, and illustrate the importance of Statute Law by enumerating a number of instances where such provisions affect the activities of the firm;
- explain the civil and criminal court system;
- examine the procedure by which a civil case is resolved;
- note briefly the chief characteristics of the English legal system.

3.0 Divisions of the Law

The vast nature of the subject area of the law requires that it be divided into a number of separate branches. The commonly accepted divisions are firstly between **municipal** and **international law.** Municipal law is defined as the law of a nation state, while international law is concerned with the area of relationships between nation states and also the regulation of the behaviour of international organisations.

3.1 Public Law

Municipal law is further divided into **public** and **private law.** Public law is chiefly concerned with the relationship between the state and its citizens and is normally concerned with criminal, constitutional, administrative, and European community branches of the law. It deals with those matters of 'public interest' as in the prevention and treatment of criminal acts.

Public law is therefore usually concerned with offences against the state, which then reflects the manner in which such cases are usually designated - the **state** (*Rex* or *Regina* in U.K.) v. the **individual.** Such proceedings are known as prosecutions the outcome being the proof of the guilt or innocence of the **defendant.** When the accused is guilty as charged the outcome is punishment of the offender.

3.2 Private Law

Private or **civil law** is concerned with relations between individuals in society, and covers such matters as the law relating to contracts, civil wrongs (torts), property, succession and trusts. It therefore deals with the regulation of agreements and relationships between private individuals together with the means for the settlement of disputes between the respective parties.

In civil law a case is brought by one individual (the **plaintiff**) against another (the **defendant**) before the court for its judgment in a process known as **litigation.** The role of the court in this instance is to judge the relevant merits of the case and provide a **remedy,** such as damages. Note that the function of the civil court is not the administration of punishment but rather the provision of a remedy.

4.0 The Sources of English Law

New law is created almost daily from a variety of sources. This reflects the dynamic nature of the law as it seeks to respond and adapt to changes in the social and political life of the society it serves. It is normal however that the law so created is a development of some previous point of law. It is of benefit therefore to be aware of the sources from which these changes emanate. Although most new law currently arises from either the activities of the Courts or Parliament, the roots of English law are more widely spread and include: the ancient custom of the realm, the common law, equity, the law merchant, statute law and European Community law.

4.1 Common Law

The system of common law was introduced by the Norman kings and sought to establish a body of 'good law', derived mainly from local customs and to reject those customs which led to 'bad law'. Many of the local customs were based on the Ancient Custom of the Realm which was therefore incorporated in the general body of common law. Principles were therefore established which could be applied to cases dealing with a similar problem. This was reinforced by the practice of making the decisions of the various judges binding on each other. A later formalisation of this was the introduction of the principle of *stare decisis* by which the decisions of judges sitting in higher courts are completely binding on all judges in lower courts thus establishing the binding nature of **judicial precedent.** The aim was consistency, the result was that law was made in the Courts by judges. Common law remains an important source of law in England, Wales and Northern Ireland to this day, although the role of the judges has moved from the creation of new law to the interpretation and clarification of existing law.

The provisions and the remedies of the common law were later supplemented by the concept of equity which was originally the sole province of the Court of Chancery but which has now been included in the role of the modern English court.

Finally, common law was further influenced by legal principles that had already been established by merchants in the course of their business. These rules had been originally developed in the various trading centres with the result that there was a uniform body of rules uniting these centres located in a number of countries. It has now almost wholly been absorbed into the common law of England.

4.2 Statute Law

Whilst the courts (or judges) can interpret law or establish precedent, the principal source of new law in the U.K. is now 'the Queen in Parliament'.

Statute law arises as the result of a lengthy process which takes a Bill through a number of stages, and usually revisions, in both Houses to the point when it receives Royal Assent and becomes an Act of Parliament, taking its place amongst the laws of the land. Only an Act can either overturn a previous judicial precedent or repeal an earlier Act or Acts.

Due to the pressure of time in both Houses and also the specific technical knowledge required to comment on much modern legislation, Parliament often delegates its powers to subordinate bodies to create further legislation to execute the general provisions of an Act. Such legislation will have the backing of Parliament provided it is within the original terms and intentions of an Act. This is referred to as **delegated legislation.**

4.2.1 Delegated Legislation

Generally speaking the main bodies to which the responsibility for the creation and administration of much of this legislation are Ministers of the Crown, local authorities and public corporations.

Ministers are empowered to make regulations under the relevant Act by means of a **Statutory Instrument** (S.I.), of which approximately 2,000 per annum are issued. For example the Secretary of State for Employment can issue S.I.s under the terms of the Health and Safety at Work Act (1974). The S.I. is normally the result of a process of consultation. The Minister concerned takes advice from expert bodies and individuals both within and without his department, and may also receive representations from other interested parties.

The provisions of the S.I. are subject to control from both Parliament and the courts. In Parliament it is considered by a select committee drawn from both Houses and must then lie before Parliament for 40 days, during which time it can be challenged by M.P.s before it can be enacted. It is also challengeable in the courts on the grounds of either 'unreasonableness' or being outwith the powers delegated in the Act.

Local authorities and public corporations are permitted by Parliament to create **Bye-laws** for the administration of their respective areas of responsibility.

4.3 European Community Law

This source is of growing importance because membership of the E.E.C. implies acceptance of the regulations of the Treaty of Rome. A number of pieces of recent legislation, such as the Companies Act and the Banking Act 1979, have risen as a result of the requirement on the U.K. to harmonise its law with that of the Community. U.K. courts must now adhere to directives from the Commission, and the decisions of the European Court are binding on all U.K. courts, including the House of Lords. A recent case concerning equality of pay for a woman employed by a mail order firm provided an interesting insight to the place of this additional source of law. Judges in the Court of Appeal considering the case based their decision on the provisions of Community, rather than U.K., legislation in the area.

Developments in Community law are therefore of interest to all producers since the proposals will eventually be incorporated - albeit in an amended form - in U.K. legislation.

4.4 Statutory Controls on Manufacturers

In recent years a large number of provisions relating to the duty of producers to either consumers or employees has been the subject of Parliamentary legislation. Some of the more important Acts are:

– **those dealing with consumer safety**

CONSUMER PROTECTION ACTS - under which safety standards of certain products - such as electrical appliances, cooking utensils, heating appliances, pencils and graphic instruments, toys, aerosol dispensers, cosmetic products, vitreous enamel-ware, children's clothing (hoods), prams and pushchairs, packaging and labelling of dangerous substances etc., are established. These provisions apply to the manufacturer.

CONSUMER SAFETY ACT 1978 - under which the Consumer Affairs minister has the power to ban the manufacture, distribution and/or supply of dangerous or unsafe goods. the net is therefore cast wider to include retailers. Failure to conform in both cases will lead to prosecution under criminal law and would also allow the injured party to seek civil damages.

Plus a number of other Acts dealing with more specific products, such as The Food and Drinks Act 1955 - dealing with the quality of food offered for sale; The Dangerous Drugs Act 1965 - relating to the requirement for the proper testing of such substances prior to their sale; The Public Health Acts - dealing with the disposal of refuse and effluent; and The Clean Air Acts designed to control the level of environmental pollution.

– **those dealing with the competitive position of the consumer**

THE FAIR TRADING ACT 1973 - designed to control the level of economic power that could be enjoyed by a producer. This Act created the Monopolies and Mergers Commission to deal with this issue and the Office of the Director General of Fair Trading, the remit of which was the regulation and banning of undesirable trade practices - some of which were already controlled under the Restrictive Trade Practices Act 1956.

THE TRADE DESCRIPTIONS ACTS - dealing with the description or pricing of goods and services.

THE WEIGHTS AND MEASURES ACTS - under which local authority officials were empowered to inspect equipment to ensure fair measures and weighing.

– **those dealing with the position of employees** - principally by means of the HEALTH AND SAFETY AT WORK ACT, which embraces much safety legislation created by the Factories Act 1961, the Offices, Shops and Railway Premises Act 1963 etc. As the provisions of this legislation are vast and detailed any consideration of them is well beyond the scope of this present text. Suffice to say that it places an obligation upon employers to ensure that the plant and systems; the handling, storage and transport devices; the workplace and the working environment are maintained in such a condition that they are 'safe and without risk to health'. A written safety policy must be formulated and provisions made for the welfare of employees together with instruction and training in health and safety matters.

5.0 The Administration of Justice

Whilst the task of enforcement of the system of laws falls primarily on the police, the administration of justice, whether in the civil or criminal realm is conducted in the Courts.

5.1 The Civil Courts

The structure of the civil courts is outlined in figure 6/1.

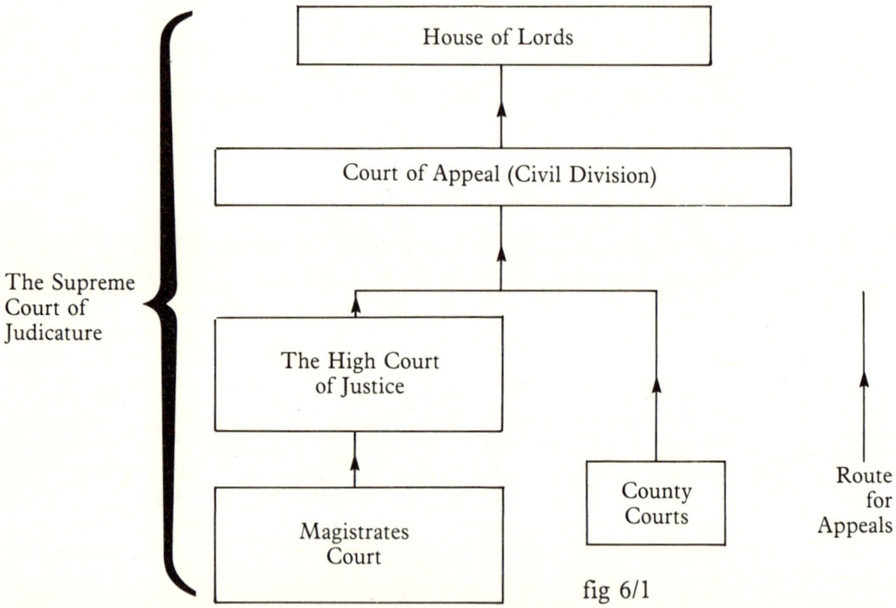

fig 6/1

The main features of the system are

– **the courts of first instance**

MAGISTRATES COURTS which deal with civil matters too trivial to be heard in High Court, such as matrimonial matters, children in care etc.

COUNTY COURTS of which there are 337, at which justice is administered by 125 circuit judges each appointed by the Lord Chancellor, and the Registrar of each County Court.

The jurisdiction of the County Court extends to disputes about contracts or torts up to a value of £2,000; equity matters to £15,000;

bankruptcies and winding up of limited companies with a share capital of less than £120,000.

Appeals from this court are made to the Court of Appeal.

HIGH COURT OF JUSTICE - hears appeals from the Magistrates Courts.

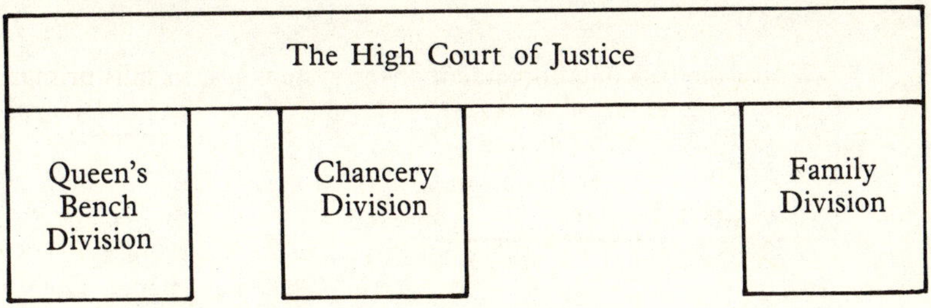

Fig. 6/2

The Queen's Bench Division which is headed by the Lord Chief Justice and staffed by 40-odd lesser or 'puisne' judges has jurisdiction over the following areas:

– tort and breach of contract;

– commercial court cases, such as insurance claims;

– Admiralty cases.

The Chancery Division deals with tax matters, the rectification, setting aside and cancellation of deeds, while the **Family Division** deals with family matters

– **the courts of appeal**

HIGH COURT OF JUSTICE - hears appeals from the County Courts.

THE COURT OF APPEAL - hears appeals from the Restrictive Practices Court established under the Restrictive Trade Practices Act, the County Courts, the High Court and tribunals.

Its membership reflects its high stature and is drawn from the Lord Chancellor, the Lord Chief Justice, the Master of the Rolls, the President of the Family division, the Lords Justice of Appeal and the Law Lords.

THE HOUSE OF LORDS is the supreme civil court for the whole of the U.K., including Scotland which has its own legal system and means of administration of justice. It is the final court of appeal and therefore its decisions are binding on all other courts in the U.K., although it does not always consider itself bound by its own decisions. It comprises the Lord Chancellor, the Lords of Appeal in Ordinary and other peers of judicial office.

5.2 The Criminal Courts

These are structured in a manner similar to the civil courts with courts of first instance and courts of appeal as illustrated in figure 6/3.

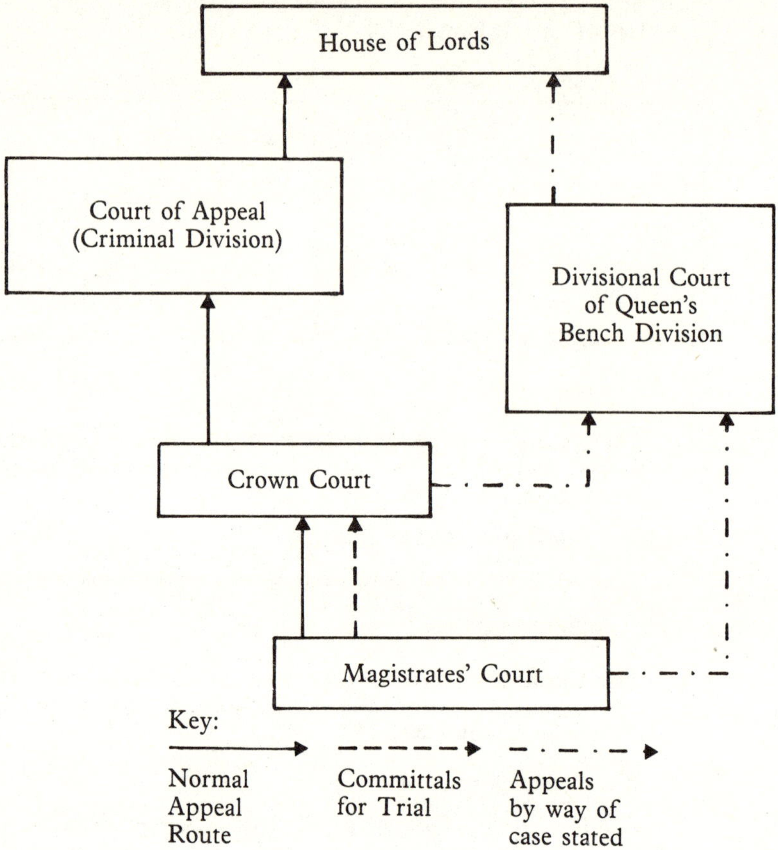

Fig. 6/3

Note again the courts of first instance and those of appeal. The Magistrates Court, which is administered by Justices of the Peace and Magistrates, is the busiest of the courts of first instance, handling approximately 98% of all criminal prosecutions in England and Wales.

The route of appeal should also be noted as well as the position of the House of Lords as the final court of appeal in the criminal system. Appeals can be made:

- against the sentence or conviction by the defendant; or
- by way of the case stated on a point of law by either the prosecution or the defendant; or
- to the House of Lords on a point of law of public importance.

5.3 Other Courts

These include

- **Administrative Tribunals,** concerned with the regulation of affairs between the citizen and the state
- **Industrial Tribunals,** concerned with employment protection legislation such as unfair dismissal, equal pay, racial and sexual discrimination; and health and safety legislation;
- the **Restrictive Practices Court;**
- the **Privy Council;** and
- the **European Court of Justice.**

5.4 Procedure

Part of the system of the administration of justice is the mechanism though which both civil disputes and criminal prosecutions are brought to court. This branch of the law is known as procedure and contains a number of points of detail. It is not intended to deal with all of these but rather to provide general guidelines of the overall process.

Civil cases commence in the office of a solicitor who will prepare the case for presentation to either the County or High Court depending on the nature of the dispute or the matter involved.

Business disputes in the County Court will normally involve the raising of an **action** by the plaintiff. Actions can either be **ordinary** or **default.** Although rules of proceedings for each are different the main stages are:

(a) the service of a summons by the aggrieved party on the party causing a breach of contract or committing a civil wrong or in default of a debt; followed by

(b) a pre-trial review of the case by the Registrar of the court at which the trial date is fixed; and

(c) the trial.

If the case falls within the jurisdiction of the High Court it will be heard in the Queen's Bench Division. In this case the procedure will be:

(a) the service of a writ on the defendant which has to be answered within 14 days;

(b) notification by the defendant within the stipulated period of his intention to defend the action;

(c) written statements of the claim and the defence are entered to the court. The claimant is allowed the right to reply to the defence entered by the defendant;

(d) a summons for directions is entered by the plaintiff to the Master to determine the future direction of the case. The Master has the power to require answers to questions posed to the parties which must be submitted on sworn affidavits;

(e) either party can then give notice of trial; leading to

(f) the trial itself, at which witnesses called by each side can be examined, cross-examined and re-examined. The process is brought to a conclusion with speeches from either counsel, a summary from the judge and the delivery of the verdict.

5.5 The Legal Profession

In the previous sections the role of the judiciary in the administration of the legal system has been described. The intention in this section is to outline briefly the distinction in role and practice between solicitors and barristers in England and Wales.

Solicitors are often described as the general practicioners of the legal profession. They are its public face, the branch of the profession with which the public comes in contact. They therefore provide a wide range of services from the preparation of cases for court to the conveyancing in respect of the purchase and sale of land, dealing principally in non-contentious work. They have limited rights to appear in certain courts, but often delegate that responsibility to a barrister.

Barristers on the other hand are specialists. Their specialism is advocacy - i.e. the representation of clients in court. Barristers alone have the right to appear before the higher courts although in practice they often are appointed by solicitors even when the solicitor has the right to appear in a particular court. In addition barristers often specialize in a particular field of law and may therefore be approached to give an opinion on the matters falling within their specialism.

Barristers are required to operate as sole practicioners, in contrast to solicitors who can operate in partnerships, and must have cases referred to them by solicitors either for an opinion or to appear in court. They cannot have direct contact with the general public. If a solicitor does refer a case to a barrister his client will then be required to pay two fees. This decision therefore will normally be taken only when the specialized services or knowledge of a barrister are deemed to be necessary.

6.0 Characteristics of English Law

English law forms the basis of the legal systems covering approximately one-third of the peoples of the world. Other systems have been derived from sources as ancient as those of English law - such as those based on Roman law, or as the result of more recent events - such as Soviet law. In addition those countries which have adopted the English system have also modified its provisions to reflect their own experience and development, as is the case for example of the U.S.A.

The chief characteristics of the English legal system are:

1 **the continuous growth of the common law.** The relatively settled development of English history from the time of the Norman kings - that is in contrast to affairs on the Continent of Europe - allowed a steady development in the formation and growth of the legal system. Even through times of revolution - either political or industrial - there was a continuity in the creation of law that could be traced to an earlier era. The nations experiencing political upheaval in Europe more often than not adopted a system of laws reflecting the political and sociological views of the victors.

2 **the absence of codification,** i.e the systematic collection of laws arranged to avoid inconsistency and overlapping. This however is not absolute as the Bills of Exchange Act 1882 and the Companies Acts demonstrate. More recently, and partly as a consequence of membership of the E.E.C., greater codification has taken place. Examples include the Banking Acts of 1979 and 1987, the Financial Services Act 1986 and the Consumer Protection Act 1987.

3 **the role of the judiciary.** The independence of the judiciary from either party to a dispute or from political interference is necessary in order to provide impartial interpretation and application of the law. As has been noted in an earlier section the part played by judges in the creation of the law in its earlier development was crucial. Judges therefore formed or moulded the common law, and although their influence nowadays is far more limited they still have a role in the interpretation of statute law and the development of common law. The doctrine of judicial precedent based on the principle of stare decisis makes the decisions of higher courts binding on lower courts as a means of achieving consistency of decisions.

4 **the independence of the legal profession.** Solicitors and barristers are 'self-employed' either on their own account or in partnership with others. They are therefore not appointed by the state and are not subject to direct political control. They are divided into the two branches discussed earlier, each being controlled by independent bodies responsible for the maintenance of standards in the profession of education, training and professional conduct. The relationship with the client is deemed to be confidential and is protected by privilege in that a member of the profession cannot be forced to disclose information to which he has become privy during the course of dealings with a client.

5 **the influence of procedure** as noted above in section 5.4

6 **no reception of Roman Law.** The development of English common law was largely unaffected by the influence of Roman Law.

6.1 Roman Law

The influence of Roman Law has marked the development of European and Scots law. Its provisions have grown in importance since the entry of the U.K. to the European community. Its chief characteristics are firstly, its view of law as a rule of conduct based on the twin concepts of justice and morality. Laws are derived from these bases for application to circumstances demanded by a modern world, and in theory should be adaptable to any set of circumstances. And secondly, as a corollary of this approach, there has been greater codification of the law in order to remove or prevent inconsistencies and areas of overlap.

6.2 Law in the U.S.A.

The legal system of the United States is based on the English system of common law. A number of modifications however have been introduced from the period of independence to the present day.

i) the Constitution is viewed as 'fundamental law', that is it is unchangeable, and is the point to which all disputes are ultimately referred;

ii) the creation of legislation emanates from both federal and state legislatures instead of the unitary system in operation in the U.K.;

iii) the judiciary is also organised on a state and federal basis;

iv) the training of the members of the legal profession is based on a 'school' system based in the American universities and does not distinguish between solicitors and barristers, all members of the profession being described as lawyers. Another notable feature is the large number of lawyers employed by U.S. industry rather than in legal practice.

7.0 Summary and Conclusion

In this chapter we have noted that in general the principal sources of law in the U.K. are the Common Law, created by the Courts and Statute Law, created by Parliament. It was noted however that the role of the modern Court in the English system is usually restricted to the interpretation, clarification of statute law, and in some cases the amendment of existing law.

Whether the law is created by Court or Parliament, the responsibility for the administration of justice falls upon the judiciary. The organisation of the Courts is divided into the administration of the civil and criminal law. Either branch has a different system of courts for the resolution of disputes between individuals in the civil law, and the prosecution of offenders under the criminal law. As procedure is of some importance in English law, the procedure associated with a civil case was examined in outline as a guide to the various stages invoved in the provision of a remedy by the court.

Finally, we examined briefly the salient points of the English legal system, contrasting them with those of other important systems.

In conclusion, it was stated in an earlier section that the the law may form part of the overall risk management strategy of the business enterprise. The process of the identification and control of the risks arising from the legal environment demands a knowledge of the provisions of the law, whether these arise out of a statutory duty - as in the case of the rules under the Health and Safety at Work Act 1974 - or under the common law. The aim of this chapter has been to provide a background to the more detailed discussion of the next two chapters.

Chapter Seven

THE LEGAL ENVIRONMENT — Elements of the Law of Contract

1.0 Key Points

The purpose of this chapter is to provide a brief introduction to the law of contract by

- an examination of the elements vital to a contract;
- noting the different forms a contract may take;
- identifying the rules surrounding the constitution of a contract;
- noting the distinction between contract terms and representations;
- examining the provisions in both common and statute law that exist to control the content of contract conditions and warranties;
- examining the provisions of the law of contract dealing with misrepresentation and breach of contract;
- surveying the range, format and distinctiveness of business contracts;
- exploring the principles of one type of business contract, the insurance contract.

2.0 Constitution of a Contract

As has been noted in the previous chapter, contracts form the basis of all business agreements. Although it was originally believed that contracts should be enforced without regard to the bargaining position of either party, legislation such as the Sale of Goods Act and the Unfair Contract Terms Act was eventually introduced to provide protection for those participating in a contract who otherwise could have been disadvantaged by virtue of a weaker bargaining position. Notwithstanding these provisions the basic elements of contract remain unchanged and are extremely important. Some familiarity with the basic elements of contract is therefore required, with reference being made to the appropriate source for more detailed information as demanded by circumstances.

2.1 Essentials of Contract

A contract is defined as:

'an agreement between two or more people which is intended to create legal obligations enforceable in the Courts'.

The contract itself comes into existence as the result of an offer being made and accepted. The rules concerning the making of offers and acceptances are examined below in section 2.2.

From the above definition a number of criteria essential to a valid contract emerge:

1 **there must be two or more parties to the contract;**

2 **the parties concerned must have entered freely into the contract of their own volition.** Contracts arising as the result of unfair or undue pressure being brought to bear on one of the parties to sign (referred to as undue influence or duress) can be set aside by a Court;

3 ***consensus in idem*** i.e. both or all parties must be in agreement as to the exact nature of the contract. The terms of the contract, whether verbal or written, must therefore be certain and capable of describing the nature of the contract. *Consensus in idem* may fail therefore as the result of mistake or misrepresentation;

4 **there must be the intention to create a legal obligation,** which implies that the contract involves either valuable consideration or the performance of a deed. The obligations under the contract are described as rights and duties, each right held by one party placing a corresponding duty on the other party;

5 **the contract must be possible to carry out,** i.e. it should not be illegal, contrary to public policy or impossible to perform;

6 **the parties must have the necessary legal capacity or power to enter into contracts.** Note that business organizations such as companies, corporations or partnerships rarely lack this power. Greater care has to be exercised with persons and associations.

These various elements have to be present in order for a contract to be valid and enforceable. Otherwise they are either

voidable - where the contract can be set aside at the instance of one or both of the parties, although if that party is willing to allow the contract to continue the agreement will then become binding on both parties; or

void - where the contract is deemed to be non-existent.

Contracts can be constituted either verbally, in writing or by a mixture of both. Certain contracts however have to be in writing. These are:

a) those which commonly appear in a written form although not required to do so by law. Such contracts include those appearing in a standard format as in the case of contracts in the construction and civil engineering industries; trading companies providing a service to the public such as travel agents, bus companies, vehicle rental firms etc,; and insurance contracts;

b) those required by law to be wholly in writing, such as agreements under the Consumer Credit Act 1974 or marine insurances;

c) those which have to be evidenced in writing by law, such as contracts relating to guarantees or the sale disposition of land;

d) those required by law to be in the form of a deed, such as conveyances of land or transfers of U.K. registered ships.

2.2 Offer and Acceptance

As we have seen a valid contract confers rights and obligations upon the respective parties. The existence of the contract however is determined by the rules pertaining to offer and acceptance, which are intended to identify whether an offer has been made or an acceptance given.

2.2.1 Offer

The rules concerning offers are as follows:

1) the terms, whether verbal or written, must be clear and should be communicated to the offeree, whether this be a specific person or the world at large. In certain instances, such as an invitation to trade or the supply of information as in the case of goods on display in a shop or in an advert, or a statement of intention, what may at first appear to be an offer would not qualify as such as the offeror is in fact inviting others to make offers to him.

2) an offer need not last an indefinite period of time. It will cease to exist under the following circumstances:

   a) the offeror recalls or revokes the offer before the acceptance is communicated; or
   b) the offer is rejected; or
   c) the offeree makes a counter-offer; or
   d) following the lapse of a certain period of time which can either be a specified period or dependent on the nature of the trade in which the offeror is involved; or
   e) upon the death of the offeror.

2.2.2 Acceptance

Acceptances can be made either verbally, in writing or by implication such as in the fulfillment of a condition.

The conditions attaching to a valid acceptance are that

a) it must fit the offer;

b) it must be communicated by the same means as the offer was made. Therefore it can be communicated by word of mouth, by telephone or telex, implied by the contract or be in writing. Acceptances in writing are deemed to have been made from the moment of posting.

2.3 Qualifications to offer and acceptance

These simple rules of offer and acceptance are qualified by a number of conditions, namely that consent of both parties to the contract should have been freely given, that the contract itself is not illegal and that it has not been subject to a mistake of fact.

2.3.1 Consent

Consent to the contract must be given freely by both parties. Evidence of threatened violence or undue influence - whereby one party takes advantage of a special relationship existing between himself and the other, such as parent-child or solicitor-client - renders a contract voidable.

2.3.2 Illegality

Illegality of contracts whether at common law such as crime, a civil wrong or an immoral act; or by statute law as in the case of gaming and wagering agreements and restrictive trade practices at all times renders a contract void.

2.3.3 Mistake

Mistakes of fact render a contract void. Note that this provision is restricted to mistakes of fact and not to those of the law because knowledge of the law is presumed. Mistakes can either be common, mutual or unilateral.

A **common mistake** occurs where both parties to the contract are mistaken about the same thing, for example where an antique dealer sells an item of furniture to a collector which they both mistakenly believe to a Chippendale.

A **mutual mistake** arises where the parties are at cross purposes, for example if a contract for the sale of a gold ring does not specify whether the gold will be 18 or 24 carat, then both parties may have different expectations of the contract.

A **unilateral mistake** occurs where one of the parties makes a mistake of which the other is aware. Additionally the party aware of the mistake may be responsible for it, in which case fraudulent misrepresentation would have taken place.

2.4 Misrepresentation

Misrepresentation - where a false statement made by one party with the intention of inducing the other to enter a contract and is successful in doing so - is a special case of mistake because the representations that are made do not form part of the contract but may be influential on the decision of the other party. Generally speaking misrepresentations must be 'positive' i.e. made rather than implied, except in the case of insurance contacts when the non-disclosure of certain facts may be construed as misrepresentation. The normal effect is to render the contract that has been entered into on the strength of the misrepresentations void.

Misrepresentation comes in four forms

- innocent - where the misrepresentation has been honest with reasonable grounds for believing its truth;
- fraudulent - where the statement has been made knowingly and dishonestly;

- non-disclosure - as in contracts of utmost good faith or a fiduciary relationship;
- negligent - where the statement is made honestly but without reasonable grounds for believing its truth.

3.0 Terms

The terms of a contract comprise conditions and warranties which can be either expressed or implied and may be verbal, written or a combination of both. The terms are distinguished from representations in that whilst the latter may be statements made during the course of a discussions or negotiations they do not form part of the contract and are therefore not binding.

3.1 Conditions and Warranties

Conditions and warranties can be implied either from trade custom and practice, the common law or from an Act of Parliament such as the Sale of Goods Act 1979 or the Unfair Contract Terms Act 1977.

Conditions are of greater importance than warranties as a breach of condition is sufficient to allow one party to end the contract and sue for damages, whereas a breach of warranty does not, although the party harmed by the breach would be entitled to sue for damages.

3.2 Unfair Contract Terms

The introduction stated that the normal practice in the law of contract was to assume that both parties are equal in terms of their respective bargaining positions. However this may not be the case for a variety of reasons. A party signing a standard form of contract that has been developed for use in a particular trading environment may not be aware of the conditions being imposed on him by the mere act of accepting an offer and concluding a contract. Failure to read the 'fine print' is not usually accepted as a defence in this situation.

Occasionally the party in a stronger bargaining position in a contract may seek to introduce certain conditions into a standard form of contract that would have the effect of reducing or restricting the rights of the other party to the contract. Examples would include attempts to avoid responsibility for certain actions by exclusion of liability clauses or seeking to deprive the weaker party of their right to sue for breach of contract or warranty thus denying them their rights at common law. The Courts and Parliament have sought to control the use of such conditions by placing conditions on the use and terms that can be included. Provided these conditions are satisfied the exclusions inserted by one of the parties will become binding on the other.

The conditions are as follows:

- **the writing which contains the clause must be a contractual document.** This excludes receipts for money but includes receipts for goods and extends to cover such items as receipts for left luggage, car parking tickets, tickets for carriage of goods plus many more similar examples;

- **reasonable steps have to be taken to bring the terms to the notice of the other party.** Reasonable notice implies merely that existence of the terms has been brought to the attention of the other party either before or at the time of the signing of the contract except in the exclusions of death or injury where the notification must be sufficiently prominent for the party signing to have seen it before the contract was signed. Signature of a document implies agreement to the terms of the exclusion clauses whether or not these have been read;
- **ambiguities in the terms of the exclusion will always be interpreted in favour of the party to whom the exclusion applies;**
- **the exclusion clause cannot be used to protect a third party;**
- **the application of the doctrine of fundamental breach.** In other words the exclusion will not apply if the party relying on it fails to fulfill the basic requirements of the contract.
- **satisfaction of the terms of the Unfair Contract Terms Act 1977.** To this point the general provisions of the law of contract have been employed to circumvent inequitable exclusion clauses. Parliament has also intervened in the form of the above Act to clarify a number of provisions that existed in other Acts and establish restrictions on the extent of liability that could be lawfully transferred by means of contractual terms. The provisions, which apply to the supply of goods and services, contracts of employment and the occupiers of premises or land, are that (a) liability for death or personal injury cannot be excluded by contract terms and (b) that attempts to exclude liability for any other kind of loss or damage will be subject to a 'test of reasonableness'.

  It should be noted, however, that the Act does not extend to insurance contracts.

4.0 Discharge and Remedy

Discharge refers to the process by which the rights and obligations that are created by a contract are extinguished. A remedy is sought if one of the parties fails to fulfill the obligations due by them under the contract.

4.1 Discharge

The normal fashion by which a contract is discharged is by the **performance** of the obligations arising out of the contract. Only the party fulfilling the obligations as required in the contract is discharged in this manner. This party can also recover his right from the other party in the event of non-fulfillment on their part. As noted this right is conditional on complete fulfillment of the obligation except in the following circumstances:

- divisible contracts;
- where partial performance has been accepted;

- where the contract has been substantially although not literally fulfilled;
- where a party is prevented from being able to complete the obligation.

Obligations may also be discharged by **express agreement** where (a) both parties have rights to surrender as in the case of bilateral discharge; or (b) where only one party has rights to surrender - unilateral discharge.

The other instances by which a contract can be discharged are:

- **frustration,** whereby a contract becomes impossible to fulfill as the result of Governmental interference, the destruction or non-availability of the subject-matter, the non-availability of a person, the non-happening of an event or if a contract entered into becomes illegal after the date of the contract. In the event of discharge through frustration any prepaid moneys are normally recoverable. This form of discharge is not available however in the case of an insurance contract.
- **breach of contract,** which may arise from either the non-performance, defective performance or untruth as regards a term of the contract, the remedies for which are discussed below.

4.2 Remedy for Breach of Contract

The fact that any contract has to be enforceable at law is designed to protect the party suffering loss as the result of breach by the other party. The remedies that are available under the law of contract operate on the principle of compensation for the aggrieved party rather than the punishment of the party failing to meet their obligations. The following remedies are available to the aggrieved under common law:

- **repudiation,** by which the contract is treated as ended. This remedy would only be available for a breach of condition;
- **action for damages,** i.e. seek monetary compensation for the breach of the contract. Note that, in keeping with the principle enunciated above, the purpose of an award of damages is to place the aggrieved party in the position he would have been had the contract been fulfilled. Damages are available for either a breach of condition or warranty. The amount that is claimed can either be for a pre-determined amount (liquidated damages), an amount to be determined by the court (unliquidated damages) or for *quantum meruit* - where the claim is made for what has already been performed under the contract.

Some other remedies which are non-monetary are available under equity and include:

- specific performance, whereby the party responsible for the breach is required to complete the action required by the contract, for example deliver an antique as originally agreed;

	Sale of Goods Contracts	Contracts of Exchange	Conditional Sale Agreement	Hire-Purchase Contracts	Credit Sale	Work & Materials Contracts	Contracts of Employment	Mortgages	Contracts for the Sale etc. of Land
Act governing contract	Sale of Goods Act 1979	—	Consumer Credit Act 1974	Consumer Credit Act 1974	Consumer Credit Act 1974	—	*Partly* Employment Protection (Consolidation) Act 1978	Law of Property Act 1925	Law of Property Act 1925
Formalities required	None	None	Written agreement under 1974 Act	Written agreement under 1974 Act	Written agreement under 1974 Act	None	Only statement of main terms under 1978 Act	Deed by 1925 Act	Evidence in writing by 1925 Act
Terminology	Seller/ buyer	—	Owner-seller/ buyer	Owner/ hirer	Seller/ buyer	Employer/ contractor	Employer/ employee	Mortgagor/ mortgagee	Vendor/ purchaser
Price	Whole price in money	Exchange value	Instalments	Instalments	Instalments	Usually by instalments but sometimes whole price	Wages or salary periodically	Mortgage instalments	10% on exchange of contract rest at conveyance stage

Delivery	Usually immediately or as agreed by parties	Usually immediately or as agreed by parties	Usually immediately or as agreed subject to conditions	Usually immediately or as agreed by parties	Usually immediately or as agreed by parties	When work is complete	—	—	Land transferred at conveyance stage
Passing of title or ownership in property	When parties intend it to (usually immediately) apply s18 rules to find that intention — buyer gets title	As parties agree but usually immediately on exchange	When condition has been met by buyer. Seller retains title until then	Hirer does not become owner until (a) all instalments paid and/or (b) conditions met and/or (c) exercise of option to purchase title with finance co. till then	When parties intend it to (usually immediately) — buyer gets title	On completion of work usually or as agreed between parties	—	Land remains in ownership of mortgagor, mortgagee merely has security over property	At conveyance stage

Table 7/1

Source: Bradley and Clark: *The Legal Environment*

- injunction, whereby the party could be compelled either to do an act or be restrained from carrying out an act.

The right to proceed against the other party does not exist indefinitely. Actions have to be raised within 6 years of the breach, the period prescribed by the Limitations Act 1980.

Finally certain remedies are specified by statute and include those available under the Sale of Goods Act 1979 - applicable only to sale of goods contracts; the Consumer Credit Act 1974 - applicable to consumer credit agreements regulated by the Act, it preserves existing remedies and additionally provides for some specialized remedies; and the Employment Protection (Consolidation) Act 1978 - applicable to contracts of employment.

4.3 Remedy for Misrepresentation

In section 2.4 it was stated that, in general, representations are not usually deemed to be terms of the contract. However if they could on some occasions be interpreted as such, then the remedies for a breach of warranty or condition arising from a misrepresentation would apply.

In the absence of this remedy, then the aggrieved party in the case of innocent, negligent or fraudulent misrepresentation could seek either damages or recission of the contract as specified by the terms of the Misrepresentation Act 1967.

Recission, which allows the innocent party to end the contract, is an equitable remedy which is available only if both the parties could revert to a pre-contract state of affairs and is not an automatic right in the same manner as repudiation.

The extent of **damages** will depend on whether the misrepresentation was innocent or fraudulent. If it was innocent or negligent then damages will be set according to those ruling for contracts. Fraudulent misrepresentation or negligent mistatement are actually forms of tort (which will be considered in the next chapter) with the result that damages awarded will be tort damages which are usually greater than those for contract.

5.0 Business Contracts

It was asserted in the introduction to chapter 8 that contracts form the basis of all business agreements. They can be verbal, written or a combination of both; in standard format with industry-wide agreed standard clauses, specifically negotiated or a blend of both. They cover a wide range of agreements from sales of goods to employment contracts, come in a large variety of formats and are regulated by a number of different Acts of Parliament in addition to the normal rules of contract. Table 7/1 on pages 108 and 109 is an attempt to summarise the distinctions between the main forms of business contract.

5.1 Insurance Contracts

Contracts of insurance are of particular interest to the risk manager as they have traditionally been the most common risk financing tool. It is only the intention, however at this stage, to give an indication of the principle elements of an insurance contract as another text is devoted to this subject area.

Insurance contracts are governed by the principles of:

- utmost good faith
- insurable interest
- indemnity
- proximate cause
- subrogation
- contribution

5.1.1 Utmost good faith

Although contracts are normally *caveat emptor,* i.e. let the buyer beware, the utmost good faith nature of an insurance contract places a duty on the insured to make full disclosure to the underwriter of all the material circumstances. The main difficulty therefore is in determining what is material. At present the test which is applied in the courts is that a fact will be regarded as material if it would influence the judgment of a prudent insurer in the acceptance and rating of the risk. For example, in the case of fire insurance the materials used and the nature of the construction of a building and its use will be material facts as would be the medical history of an insured person in the case of life insurance.

There are certain instances where disclosure is not required as the insurer is deemed to be in possession of the full facts such as the facts of law, facts which lessen the risk, facts about which the insurer has been put on enquiry, facts which the insurer's survey should have noted and facts covered by the policy conditions.

The remedies for innocent breaches of this principle such as non-disclosure or innocent misrepresentation are similar to those in a conventional contract. Likewise the remedies for fraudulent breaches as in the case of concealment or fraudulent misrepresentation.

5.1.2 Insurable interest

Insurable interest is the **financial** interest of the insured in the house/ship/car etc, which is referred to as the subject matter of the insurance.

'What is it that is insured in a fire policy; Not the bricks and materials used in building the house, but the interest of the insured in the subject matter of insurance.' from CASTELLAIN v PRESTON (1833)

This implies that there must be property, rights, interests, life, limb, or potential liability capable of being insured; that these must be the subject matter of the insurance; and that the insured must be in such a relation with the subject matter, recognized at law, that he benefits from its safety, well-being or freedom from liability and would be damaged by its damage or by the existence of any liability.

Legislation from the 18th to 20th centuries has reinforced the necessity of the existence of insurable interest in a valid policy of insurance.

5.1.3 Indemnity

Indemnity has been described as 'the controlling principle in insurance law'. It is a principle by which the insured is provided with financial compensation sufficient to place him in the same financial position as he was before the loss occurred. It is closely linked to insurable interest since it is this that is insured, which means that any payments made cannot exceed this interest.

For example in the case of property the amount paid to an insured in the event of a loss is value at the date and place of loss, not the original cost. No allowance is to made for consequential loss or loss of sentimental value. In the event of a machine being replaced by a newer machine a deduction in respect of wear and tear has to be made in order to maintain the principle of indemnity. In the case of loss of money or loss arising out of liability the exact amount can be determined by accountants in the case of consequential loss or by the Court in the case of liability.

Many policies may contain a modification of the indemnity principle by means of a policy wording, a common example being found in the 'new for old' clauses in the domestic household policy, which provides for reinstatement rather than indemnity.

The extent of the indemnity can be limited by the insurer by fixing a limit to the sum insured or by the application of the 'average', whereby the value of indemnity is limited to the proportion of the sum insured divided by the full value of the subject matter of the insurance, thus giving rise to the danger of under-insurance. The assumption of a voluntary excess or deductible by the insured also contributes to a reduction of the amount of indemnity.

Indemnity is provided in the form of cash payments, repair, replacement, or reinstatement.

5.1.4 Proximate cause

Losses often arise from more than a single cause. The problem then is to decide whether the loss falls within the scope of the policy cover. Provided the insured can demonstrate that the loss arose from a peril which was covered by the policy and that the outcome arose from the natural course of events following the original cause, then the loss will fall within the policy cover.

This implies that firstly, the risk insured against must actually take place; secondly that damage to the subject matter due to attempts to minimise a loss already taking place would also be covered; and finally that where the occurrence of the original peril has meant that the loss was inevitable, even although it was not the actual event that led to the loss, this also will be covered.

5.1.5 Subrogation

Subrogation is defined as the right of one person to stand in the place of another and to avail themselves of all the rights and remedies of that other, whether already enforced or not. Thus an insurer having indemnified a person is entitled to receive back from the insured anything he may receive from any other source. Note that if an insured who has already claimed on a policy recovers funds from a source other than the insurer, the money is not his but is effectively being held in trust for the insurer.

Subrogation therefore can only exist where the contract is one of indemnity which also ensures that the insurer is not entitled to any more than he has paid out to the insured.

5.1.6 Contribution

Contribution operates to preserve the principle of indemnity by ensuring that the insured cannot be paid twice over for the same loss even although the same subject matter may be insured with different insurers.

It arises when two or more policies of indemnity exist which cover the same or common interest, peril giving rise to loss or subject matter and each policy is liable for the loss.

It means that each insurer is liable only for the rateable proportion of the loss, i.e. in proportion to overall liability and that it is the right of an insurer to call upon others similarly liable to the same insured to share the cost of an indemnity payment.

6.0 Summary and Conclusion

The subject matter of this chapter has been the law of contract, a working knowledge of which, it was argued, is essential since all business agreements draw upon the rules of contract. It has examined the elements vital to the constitution and enforcement of a valid contract such as the necessity for two or more parties, that the parties concerned must have entered freely into the contract of their own volition, that both or all parties must be in agreement as to the exact nature of the contract, that there must be the intention to create legal obligations, that the contract must be possible to carry out not being illegal, contrary to public policy or impossible to perform and finally that the parties must have the necessary legal capacity or power to enter into contract. This examination has highlighted some of the matters that could prevent the creation of a valid contract such as duress, illegality, mistake and misrepresentation.

The manner in which contracts arise through the rules of offer and acceptance were considered as were the different forms which a contract could take. It was noted that while all contracts do not have to be in writing to be considered valid, there are some which do and others which by trade custom and practice also take this form. The development of mutually agreed standard forms of contract within certain industries means that those participating in these should be aware of the particular demands of each standard contract. The existence of such forms of contract has raised the problem that those not familiar with their terms may be placed at a disadvantage in the contractual situation. To that end protection for these parties has been evolved both in common and statute law to control clauses that may be inserted in a contract, in particular those which seek to remove liability for death and personal injuries.

The distinction between representations and the terms of a contract were also noted together with the provisions which allowed a party whose interest had been damaged by misrepresentation or breach of contract to seek the appropriate remedy either in the form of monetary compensation as in damages or in the form of an injunction or the repudiation of the contract.

Finally one particular form of contract, the insurance contract, was examined in a more detail than the others as it remains one of the main forms of spreading the cost of risk.

In conclusion, an awareness of the law of contract may be employed in one of two main ways:

- defensively as a means to identify potential sources of risk; and
- offensively as part of the strategy of the control of risk by seeking to transfer or reduce exposure to risk by means of contract terms other than insurance, provided these terms are in accord with the provisions of the Unfair Contract Terms Act.

Chapter Eight

THE LEGAL ENVIRONMENT — Elements of the Law of Tort

1.0 Key Points

The purpose of this chapter is to

- discover the meaning of tort and the range of different forms of torts that exist;
- examine the nature and circumstances of the different liabilities that arise under tort;
- note the different forms of remedy available to a person who has suffered in tort;
- note the general defences that may be employed by a person facing an action in tort from another;
- examine the specific tort of negligence in a little detail.

2.0 Nature of Tort

The business enterprise is surrounded by the provisions of the law of tort. Any organisation which has incurred liabilities in respect of employers liability, products or public liability has encountered this area of law.

2.1 Definition

According to Lord Denning, 'the province of tort is to allocate responsibility for injurious conduct'. Tort therefore is concerned with **civil** rather than criminal **wrongs,** and refers to 'harm' suffered by a person whether that be injury to his person or character, financial loss or interference to his rights to enjoy his property.

2.2 Contrast

The nature of tort is perhaps best explained by contrast with contract and criminal law.

2.2.1 Contract

SOURCE: tort arises from an infringement of the rules of civil law existing under statute and common law whereas any action in contract must arise as the result of a breach of the terms of a contract.

RIGHTS & DUTIES: rights and duties in tort are therefore derived from civil law rather than the terms of contract.

REMEDIES: these usually take the form of damages or injunction, which is a fewer number than those available under contract. In tort however an award of damages may also be given with the intention of punishing the defendant.

2.2.2 Criminal law

Tort is a civil rather than a criminal wrong. It arises out of an action brought by an individual rather than the state as in the case of criminal law, the outcome of which is an award of damages against the defendant rather than the imposition of a punishment.

2.2.3 Summary

A tort can involve a breach of contract, a criminal wrong or both and is either a civil wrong remediable at law or the breach of a duty that has been fixed by law. In summary therefore where one person suffers unlawful harm or damage at the hands of another, an action in tort for that damage or injury arises.

2.3 Forms of Tort

Many forms of tort require proof of damage or loss before they are actionable; some, such as libel or trespass, do not require proof and are therefore actionable in themselves - torts *per se.*

The main forms of tort are:

- **negligence,** which has been defined as 'the omission to do something which a reasonable man ... would do, or doing something which a prudent and reasonable man would not do';
- **liability of occupiers of premises,** which is the subject of the Occupiers' Liability Act 1957;
- **strict liability,** which arises whether a person was at fault or not and often involves the breach of regulations under an Act of Parliament like the Health and Safety at Work Act 1974;
- **trespass to property,** or 'the unlawful interference with the rights of another'. This tort is intended as a protection for the possessor of property, whether that be land or goods. The rights in question in trespass are therefore those of the possessor, not necessarily the owner of the property;
- **nuisance** is an unlawful act or omission which interferes a person's use of his property or affects his health, comfort or convenience. This is known as private nuisance. Public nuisance is similar except that it interferes or endangers the common rights of the public and that it is normally treated as a criminal wrong;
- **defamation,** which can take either the form of libel or slander, is the injuring of a persons's reputation by means of the publication of a false statement for which there is no lawful justification;
- economic torts such as **conspiracy, deceit** or **injurious falsehood.** Conspiracy occurs when two or more persons collude without lawful justification to harm the interests of a third party. Deceit or fraud is an example of fraudulent misrepresentation which

was dealt with in the previous chapter. Injurious falsehood is distinguished from conspiracy or defamation because it is directed against the business interests rather than the reputation of the person concerned.

Finally it should be noted that, in certain instances the law may not provide a remedy for harm suffered by one person as the result of another's actions. This is known as damage without legal wrong, its most common occurrence being in the field of ordinary trade competition. For example the proprietor of a small DIY shop being forced out of business as the result of the opening of a branch of large wholesale DIY trading concern on his doorstep.

3.0 Liability

Generally speaking any legal person of full age and contractual authority can sue or be sued in tort. The definition of legal person extends to cover forms of business organisation such as partnerships and limited companies.

A limited company has full power to sue in its own name and be held responsible for the actions of its agents or servants except where their actions were outwith the powers of the company or if they were undertaken without the express authority of the company. Partners are jointly and severally liable for torts committed by each other provided the actions concerned are in the ordinary course of business.

There are special provisions relating to loss or damage caused by certain public bodies or officials in the course of their duties. For example, individual policemen are exempted for liability for any tort committed in the course of their duties, the chief police officer of the area in this case assumes vicarious liability for the actions of his officers. Similarly, the employees of local authorities and hospitals enjoy exemption from tortious liability. These bodies which have full legal personality are vicariously liable for the acts of their servants. The Post Office still retains immunity from any tort arising from damage or loss as the result of loss or delay in the post unless the package concerned has been registered.

3.1 Vicarious Liability

In the above section it was indicated that there were certain occasions when one person would become responsible for the torts of another. This is known as vicarious liability. The main areas in which this arises are:

- **principal and agent.** One of the main provisions of the law of agency is that provided the agent acts within the authority delegated to him by the principal, or if actions originally outwith the principal's instructions are subsequently ratified by him, the principal is vicariously liable for all acts undertaken by the agent on his behalf.

- **master and servant.** In general a master is vicariously liable for the torts of his servant, provided they are conducted in the course of his or her employment. The crucial element is therefore whether the relationship is one of master and servant. Whilst no rules have been established by the courts, a number of guidelines have bee indicated, namely that a servant is one who has voluntarily entered into a contract of service with the employer, who has the power to select, appoint or dismiss, in return for the payment of salary or wages.

- **independent contractors.** An independent contractor works under a contract for services and has freedom in deciding the manner and timing of the work which has been contracted to him. Generally therefore the employer of a sub-contractor has no vicarious liability for torts committed by him, except in the following circumstances:

  ⋆ where the employer himself owes a primary duty to any plaintiff;
  ⋆ where a statute imposes an absolute duty upon a person, as in the Health and Safety at Work Act, this cannot be delegated to another;
  ⋆ where the work concerned involves hazardous operations liability cannot be delegated by employing independent contractors;
  ⋆ liability on the individual for an independent contractor under the rule in Rylands v. Fletcher (1868) - see section 3.2;
  ⋆ a master cannot escape responsibility for the duty of safety to his servants by delegating its performance to an independent contractor. He can however seek an indemnity from the contractor as part of the terms of the contract. He cannot be liable for wrongs committed by servants in the course of the contractors's employment, which is described as collateral negligence of the contractor.

3.2 Strict Liability

Strict liability differs from the normal forms of tort in that fault does not have to be proved. It is still necessary however to prove that loss or harm has occurred.

3.2.1 Breach of statutory duty

This applies mainly to the field of industrial injuries and to a great extent is concerned with the provisions of the Health and Safety at Work and related Acts dealing with safety, health, environment and practices in the workplace. These Acts impose an absolute duty which means that no proof of negligence or wrongful intent is required. It does require proof that

1 the statute has been broken;

2 the breach is the direct cause of the injury or damage;

3 the person suing is from a class of person that the statute was intended to protect; and

4 the injury is one which the statute was intended to prevent.

3.2.2 The rule in Rylands v Fletcher

The Rylands and Fletcher case concerned the construction of a water reservoir by the defendant for use in his mill. Upon filling the reservoir water escaped into mine-shafts that were present on the land and that connected to the plaintiffs mine which was on adjoining land with the effect that the mine was flooded. The rule established was that if

- there was a 'non-natural' use of the land;
- there was an escape from the defendant's land; and
- that the escape was 'likely to do mischief'

then there was a *prima facie* case for the defendant to be answerable 'for all the damage which is the natural consequence of the escape'.

Note that damage has to be proved and that the employment of a competent independent contractor cannot excuse the defendant from liability.

The rule has been held to apply to other 'escapes', for example of electricity, trees, fencing, sewage and explosives.

3.3 Occupiers Liability

A statutory duty of care was imposed upon occupiers of premises by the Occupiers Liability Act 1957 which was later extended by the provisions of the 1972 Defective Premises Act. Under these Acts an occupier, landlord or constructor of private dwellings owes a common duty of care to all visitors except in so far as he is free to and does restricts, modify, extend or exclude his duty to any visitor by agreement or otherwise. Neither builders or landlords can restrict or exclude any of the duties imposed by the Act, the powers of exclusion by other occupiers being subject to the terms of the Unfair Contract Terms Act 1977.

The duty owed by occupiers is to ensure that visitors to the premises will be reasonably safe for the duration of their presence on the premises. This duty is owed only to those visitors who have or may be deemed to have the permission of the occupier to be there. Within the restrictions given above the occupier is permitted to seek to reduce or exclude liability arising out of the duty outlined above by means of the framing or posting of a suitable notice.

4.0 Remedies

The remedies available for tort through the courts are to seek an award of damages, the imposition of an injunction or the restitution of property whereby the defendant would be required to restore certain property to the plaintiff.

4.1 Damages

Damages are monetary compensation awarded a plaintiff for civil wrongs that have been suffered and take three main forms: unliquidated damages, exemplary damages and aggravated damages which are awarded for willful and malicious conduct on the part of the defendant.

4.1.1 Unliquidated damages

The underlying principle of unliquidated damages is the restoration of the plaintiff to the pre-loss position. Unliquidated damages can either be:

GENERAL which are given when the loss cannot be determined exactly. The mere occurrence of the tort is sufficient for damages to be awarded in this case; or

SPECIAL when a specific amount is claimed by the plaintiff and by implication is calculable. Proof of loss or injury suffered by the plaintiff is required in this case.

The award of unliquidated damages may occasionally be only a nominal amount as recognition of the occurrence of an infringement of rights but from which no loss has arisen. Where loss has been suffered the award will be substantial.

4.2.1 Exemplary damages

These damages are awarded with the intention of imposing a punishment upon the defendant rather than compensating the defendant. They will only be available under the following circumstances:

- where a statute authorises the making of such an award;
- where unconstitutional, oppressive or arbitrary action by a government servant causes harm to the plaintiff;
- where the potential profit accruing from the actions of the defendant would be greater than the compensation that would have to be paid to the plaintiff.

4.1.3 Conditions for the award of damages

In order for a claim for damages to be recognised the loss that arises out of the tort must either

(a) have been forseeable; or

(b) the original act or omission giving rise to the loss has not been superceded by a subsequent event.

The point of these conditions is to decide whether a person should be liable for all the circumstances arising out of his tortious act.

With respect to the first of these conditions, the House of Lords has adopted the view of the Privy Council in a case known as the 'Wagon

Mound' (No 1) 1961 that a person can only be liable for the consequences of a negligent act or omission only if he could have reasonably forseen that these would be the result of his tortious conduct. 'Forseeability becomes that effective test'.

This point is of particular interest to those considering the implications of the provisions of the EEC Directive of 25 July 1985 which have been incorporated in the Consumer Protection Act 1987. The basic provision of the directive is to impose a strict liability upon the producer of defective products subject to a number of qualifications. Perhaps the most important of these for the producer - and the most significant in terms of consumer rights - is the provision that that there should be no liability if 'the state of scientific and technical knowledge at the time when he (the producer) put the product into circulation was not such as to enable the existence of the defect to be discovered'. This would give manufacturers a complete defence if they can demonstrate that neither they nor producers of similar products could have known that the products were dangerous. This so-called 'development risks' defence would seem to fall within the spirit of the judgment of their Lordships as noted above.

The meaning of the second condition is that if a new act following the original act or omission breaks the 'chain of causation' between the first cause and its consequences, the loss or harm suffered by the plaintiff cannot then be directly attributed to the defendant's conduct, in which case the damages would be reduced or dismissed.

4.2 Injunction

Injunctions are issued by either the County or High Court when it is satisfied that an award of damages would not be appropriate in the circumstances. The injunction can be made to compel the defendant to take a certain course in respect of a specific tort, for example remove a nuisance or prohibit the continued commission of a tort as in the case of trespass of property.

It may be issued pending the decision of the Court of the Act in question in which case it is known as an interlocutory injunction, or following the decision of the Court in favour of the plaintiff - a perpetual injunction.

An injunction prohibiting the commission of a certain action can be suspended in the short term in order to enable the defendant to comply with it over the longer term.

4.3 Limitation of Actions

Liabilities arising out of tort do not exist indefinitely. The time period in which action to seek remedy for loss or harm suffered as the result of a tort is controlled by the Limitation Act 1980. In common with contract a period of 6 years can run either from the time when the tort took place in the case of torts which are actionable *per se,* from the moment the damage took place in the case of torts actionable on proof of damage or from the discovery of a fraud or mistake by the plaintiff.

The time period of 6 years has been altered in the following instances to:

- 3 years for fatal accidents and personal injuries arising from nuisance, negligence or breach of duty;
- 2 years for life, personal injury to persons on board a vessel and damage to a vessel or her cargo;
- 30 years in respect of damage arising from nuclear incidents.

5.0 Defences Against Tort

A number of specific defences are available for particular torts but in addition there are a number of general defences which can be employed in all cases whenever appropriate.

5.1 *Volenti non fit injuria*

The principal of this defence is that no injury or harm can be done to a willing person. In other words, where a person has consented to the physical and legal risks associated with a particular activity then a tort cannot arise. Consent can be given verbally, in writing or by implication and must be given voluntarily since knowledge of the risk is not normally regarded as being sufficient. The most popular examples of this defence are drawn from the fields of sport where injuries received are not torts because the activity has been entered into voluntarily.

This principle has been employed in the area of master and servant. Where a servant on some occasions may be required to act to his danger which has arisen as the result of negligence on the part of the employer, consent in these circumstances cannot be regarded as voluntary and the defence would therefore fail. This however is never a straightforward issue.

Similarly, this defence is not applicable in situations where a party acting out of a legal or moral duty, such as in the case of a doctor or a policeman, puts himself at risk or suffers harm as a consequence of fulfilling these duties.

5.2 Mistake

Generally no allowance is made for mistakes of law - where the maxim of ignorance of the law is no excuse applies without exception, or mistakes of fact.

Mistake of fact is available as a defence only on a few occasions such as malicious prosecution or false imprisonment provided the mistake is adjudged to have been a reasonable one.

5.3 Necessity

This defence is available only when the defendant is compelled by circumstances to act to prevent a greater harm to himself, a third party or the nation and is only acceptable if the harm or damage caused is held to be reasonably justified in the circumstances.

5.4 Inevitable Accident

That is the occurrence of an event that could not have been prevented by taking reasonable precautions.

In NCB v Evans & Co and another (1951) a sub-contractor employed by Evans to cut a trench across some land damaged an electric cable which passed under the land but which was not marked on any available map, the existence of which was not known to either Evans & Co or the council that owned the land. The outcome was that as the result of the damage to the cable, water seeped in causing an explosion which interrupted electricity supplies to the colliery managed by the plaintiff. The Court of Appeal held that the defendants were entirely free from fault.

5.5 Statutory Authority

There may be occasions when legislation created by Parliament or a subordinate body such as a Minister of the Crown or a local authority authorises an alleged wrong. Provided the action is reasonable and the obligation imposed on the relevant body can be performed in no other way then this defence allows the act even though it may cause harm. This is known as absolute authority and contrasts with conditional authority which only empowers the body concerned to act on the proviso that no harm is caused to others.

5.6 Self-defence

A person is permitted to use reasonable force, which must be in proportion to the loss threatened, to defend himself or third parties against unlawful force. This defence is also available for the protection of goods or property on similar conditions that the means employed to protect must be reasonable and proportionate to the threatened loss.

5.7 Act of God

This defence is employed when injury or harm arises which no human foresight or precaution could have prevented.

6.0 Negligence

It has been decided to look a little more closely at this specific tort because it is one of the most important and common forms of tort in English law today.

Negligence can be regarded as either a state of mind which has given rise to the occurrence of a particular tort or as a tort in its own right. It is in this latter category that it is discussed below.

For the tort of negligence to exist the plaintiff must be able to prove the following:

1) that a duty of care was actually owed to him by the defendant;
2) that this duty was breached; and
3) that harm or injury to the plaintiff was the outcome of the breach of the duty.

6.1 Duty of Care

The duty of care imposes an obligation on any person to consider the consequences of his actions or of his failure to take certain action. Therefore consideration should be given as to the effect of an act or omission on persons directly or closely affected by the act or its omission. However the person responsible for the act or omission must be able to reasonably forsee the outcome of the act which raises issues which were discussed in section 4.1.3.

For example in the well-known, and perhaps well-worn, case of Donoghue V Stevenson in 1932 a person became ill through drinking a bottle of ginger-beer which contained the decomposed remains of a snail. The court held that the manufacturer was liable to the consumer in negligence even although the consumer had not purchased the liquid.

The duty of care also extends to the use of words and requires that persons guard against negligent misstatements.

The duty of care therefore exists in a wide and widening range of circumstances. There are however a number of examples where the duty is recognised to exist either because it has been statutorily imposed, recognised a. common law or where its existence is obvious from the circumstances.

6.1.1 Duty of care recognised at law

MANUFACTURERS The example of Donoghue v Stevenson above established the duty of care of the manufacturer to the consumer;

EMPLOYERS An employer owes a duty of care to his employees, and is expected to provide reasonable working conditions, both in terms of working methods and safeguards for machinery as well as competent fellow employees. Employers are obliged to maintain adequate insurances in respect of liability for physical injury or disease suffered by employees in the course of their employment. This applies even if the accident was caused by defective equipment supplied by a third party.

HIGHWAY USERS There is a duty of care to other users. This duty extends to railways, shipping and canal navigation.

PROFESSIONAL PERSONS Doctors, surgeons, dentists, surveyors, architects, accountants and other similar professional persons owe a duty of care in the discharge of their duties to those with whom they are in a professional relationship.

BAILEES The duty of care owed to the bailor to take care of the goods entrusted to the bailee arises separately from the contract of bailment under which the goods are given to the bailee.

CARRIERS Persons such as railways, bus companies and road hauliers who carry persons or freight for reward owe a duty of care to the passengers or the owners of the goods independently of the terms of the contract of transport.

6.1.2 Duty of care evident from circumstances

Or where 'the thing speaks for itself' - *res ipsa loquitur.* In cases where a duty obviously exist, only negligence has to be proved as the existence of the duty is accepted without demur.

6.2 Breach of Duty

The existence of a duty of care does not in itself settle the matter of what is a breach of that duty. This implies the recognition that a certain standard of care exists and should be honoured. The standard of care expected, however varies with the nature of the activity. For example it would be expected that the level of care exercised by an 'ordinary prudent man' in handling a walking stick would be different from that if he were handling a shotgun. Similarly, a variation in the standard of care exercised by the manufacturer of wooden pallets in contrast to that of a manufacturer of dangerous drugs and controlled substances would be expected.

Furthermore if a person sets themselves up as possessing a particular skill, then the standard of care applied is that which would be reasonably expected of a person of his professional occupation and would be greater than that expected of an 'ordinary prudent man'.

6.3 Contributory Negligence

On occasions a defendant may argue that the loss or injury suffered by the plaintiff was not solely due to his actions but that the plaintiff by virtue of the actions which he took contributed to his injury or loss. For example a person stepping negligently into the path of an oncoming vehicle that was being carelessly driven would find that the award of damages would be reduced to take account of his contribution to the accident.

The main defence that the plaintiff would have against this line of argument would be to show either that he acted on the spur of the moment - known as the 'Dilemma Principle'; or that the defendant could have forseen that the original act or omission was likely to cause this reaction by the plaintiff - known as the Doctrine of the New Act Intervening where the new act is identified as the reaction of the plaintiff to the circumstances in which he finds himself. If either of these points were accepted by the Court, the defendant would be fully liable and the award of damages would not be reduced.

7.0 Summary

The area under examination in this chapter has been the law of tort, which it was noted is the legal basis of the problems of all kinds of liability to which the business enterprise may be subject. It was seen that tort is concerned with providing a means of redress for those parties which had suffered injury, loss or harm at the hands of another. Tort itself was defined as a civil wrong which arose out of a breach of the rules of civil law which are drawn from the provisions of statute and common law.

A number of forms of tort were considered briefly as an illustration of the wide range of activities covered by this area of law.

Since tort is concerned with providing remedies for those who have suffered loss, whether or not they were in contractual relationship with the party responsible for the loss, this implies liability for the party alleged to have caused the harm. It was noted that under certain circumstances such as those of master and servant, principal and agent and the employment of independent sub-contractors, one party can become responsible for the acts of another and therefore assumes a vicarious liability. Normally the liability of the defendant arises out of a fault or negligence on the part of the defendant, but in a situation of strict liability fault did not have to exist. A breach of a statutory duty or the rule enunciated in Rylands v Fletcher was sufficient to create liability. Some consideration was given to the duties imposed upon occupiers of premises by the Act of the same name.

The main remedies of damages and injunction available in tort were considered briefly. It was noted that although the normal purpose of an award of damages was similar to that in contract there were circumstances under which the award could be designed to punish the defendant rather than simply compensate the plaintiff.

The main forms of defence against an action in tort such as volenti non fit injuria, mistake, necessity, inevitable accident, statutory authority, self-defence and Act of God were examined briefly and the circumstances of their use noted.

Finally, particular attention was given to the specific tort of negligence. The importance and the obligations of the duty of care which is owed by legal persons in a number of specific situations was considered ranging from the duty owed to other users of highways to the duty of an employer to his employees. The significance of the recognition of a standard of care to the decision as to whether or not a breach had taken place was also examined, as was the defence of contributory negligence, and the conditions under which it may be successful, which may be put up by the defendant.

8.0 Conclusion

The aim of this section on the legal environment has been to cover the material necessary to provide a working knowledge of business law. Much has not been covered, but an attempt has been made to examine those areas which it is hoped will provide the basics upon which further knowledge and understanding can be built. In accordance with this objective therefore the sources of legislation, the means and the procedures of the administration of justice, the body of law known as contract which regulates the majority of business agreements and tort, the means whereby a civil wrong can be redressed have been examined.

These areas, properly understood, will provide an appreciation of the conventions or rules which determine the manner in which business is conducted, how these change and the risks imposed by them as the result of breach, non-compliance or carelessness.

Chapter Nine

THE POLITICAL ENVIRONMENT

1.0 Introduction

The legislative framework within which organisations have to operate is a reflection of the belief and value systems of the societies within which they exist. This environment and the forces which shape it are however less precisely defined. Furthermore the same beliefs and values are not held by all members of the population. In theory therefore legislation which has to be precise and clearly and unambiguously defined is the result of a degree of unanimity between the various interest groups of the society. In practice the laws of the land will tend to reflect the views and values of the dominant section of the society, whether this dominance has arisen as the result of birth, the democratic process or other means. The source of the dominance has important implications for the manner in which change in the society originates, is controlled or is managed - implications which may have repercussions on the operation of the business enterprise.

According to Bannister and Bawcutt in *Practical Risk Management,* social and political risks arise from changes which are beyond the direct control of the organisation and to which the organisation has to respond. Social change is relatively straightforward to document but difficult to define precisely. Part of this is undoubtedly due to the long-term nature of such change even in a modern world where change is more rapid than previously and part to the invisible nature of cultural influences. The risk lies in perceiving the world as it **was** rather than it is. The discipline of Marketing is concerned with identifying these trends as a means of controlling and reducing the level of speculative risk faced by the business enterprise.

Lack of perception of such changes can be equally disastrous in the world of pure risk. For example a failure to appreciate an increased alienation from work, less concern for private property, greater expectation of provision of government services, increasing levels of violent or destructive behaviour or alteration of police strategy in dealing with crime will lead to inadequate measures for the control of property loss. Nowhere has this myopia been more evident than in the field of computer security. A computer risks survey of financial institutions revealed that 37% of exposures identified could lead to material financial loss - that is, serious enough to warrant disclosure in the annual accounts; and that in 18% of these cases there was a significant probability that loss would occur within a year.

Political risk is more amenable to identification as it is normally associated with the consequences of the action of government such as in the field of legislation or economic management. The uncertainties posed by current or future government policies constitute a sizeable threat to the majority of businesses.

Given this scenario, risk management is concerned with the identification of these threats and the initiation of the subsequent adjustments required by the forecast change in social and political environments.

In the light of the above, the definition of political and social risk framed by Lloyd in *Political Risk Management* would seem to be appropriate:

> 'all threats to the future of an organisation arising from ***human activity*** outside the organisation.'

2.0 Key Points

The main purpose of this chapter therefore is:

- to establish that the business organisation cannot exist in isolation from the socio-political environment;
- to provide a framework for identification of the areas of conflict between the business enterprise and society;
- to indicate briefly a number of sources of information about the social and political climate;
- to define the concepts of social and political instability;
- to identify the underlying factors of social and political instability
- to note a number of indicators of the above; and
- to examine the areas of interface between government and business.

3.0 Interface with the Socio-political Environment

Business cannot avoid the issues raised by social and political factors because

i) it is itself responsible in part for a changing social environment;

ii) the necessity of public acceptability; and

iii) business organisations are in themselves a microcosm of the social and political process.

3.1 A Force for Change

To survive businesses have constantly to develop new products and markets and identify new investment opportunities. In addition new technologies are adopted either for the exploitation of new markets and products or for the more efficient production of existing goods and services. Both introduce change into the lives of consumers and producers. Households have a wider range - and grow to expect a widening range - of goods from which to choose, and workers have new skills to acquire. The widening range of choice may render the original form of distribution of goods and services inappropriate to the new situation, hence the move from High street/corner shop to super and hyper-markets. The new technologies of production may render existing skills and methods of skills training obsolete and create new fields of expertise.

The overall result is change in the social and cultural environment. Change, as was noted in the first chapter, is the seedbed of risk. For example, the advent of the computer has revolutionized many production technologies but has also reduced the need for human labour, altered the skills necessary to survive in such an environment and increased the vulnerability of sensitive information to unauthorised disclosure. These changes have important implications for such matters as industrial relations, industrial espionage and fraud. An increasing level of computer literacy raises the degree of significance of such threats to confidentiality of information.

The normal activity of business therefore is continually altering the skills, habits and expectations of the population at large. These shifts can exacerbate existing trends or stimulate the development of new threats.

3.2 A Microcosm of Society

A variety of competing interests exist within business organisations, with the result that they are faced with the problems similar to those of society. The structures which have been developed are also comparable to those adopted by society to deal with the same issues, namely those of the establishment, recognition and acceptance by the members of the organisation of the source and exercise of authority and power; the existence of competing claims for its finite resources; and finally the means by which such competing claims and conflicts of interest between shareholder, employee, supplier or customer are resolved. In this sense business is an intensely political activity and cannot fail to be influenced by the environment within which the organisation is located.

The interdependence of the organisation with the environment will from time to time create points of stress for individual members as it is inevitable that in certain areas the interests of the organisation will conflict with those of society at large. The threat to the organisation is that such a conflict may provide sufficient motivation for an employee to exploit a position of trust within the organisation to its ultimate loss. Management of this area of threat necessitates an understanding of the prevailing value system of the members of the organisation.

3.3 Necessity

In the long run survival depends on the sale of the goods and services produced by the organisation. In a competitive environment this in turn rests not solely on the ability to price competitively or deliver timeously but also the public's perception of the provider of the goods or services.

This is subject to a subtle combination of influences. Obviously quality and price competitiveness are important components, but since 1945 other factors have affected the public image of the business organisation. Many of the criticisms, principally directed at multi-national corporations, such as:

a) the concentration of economic power in the hands of a non-accountable minority;

b) the use of concentrated economic power against the public interest;

c) the exploitation of workers and consumers; and

d) the diminution of the environment and quality of life;

have enjoyed a favourable reception in many quarters with the consequence that public opinion has tended to distrust the activities and motives of 'big business'.

The most revealing aspect of these criticisms is simply the recognition of a conflict of interests between these corporations and the societies within which they operate and secondly, that the organisations in question were largely unaware or unconcerned about the strength of opinion against them.

To ensure public acceptability of its goods and services however and hence assure its survival, the firm requires to be conscious of and sensitive to the impact which its operations have on the community in which it is located.

Although a long term view is at first more costly it is necessary if the organisation is to continue to compete successfully and acceptably in a particular society. According to one writer, 'the real challenge for management in the next thirty years is integrating social purpose with technical and economic progress'. In terms of the model illustrated in figure 1/1, this means the identification of the trends in the social and political spheres as a means to adjusting the stance of the firm to take account of these developments thereby reducing the intensity of the 'collisions' and permitting the firm to pursue its objectives. Failure to do so may increase the friction to such an extent that the achievement of the firm's objectives may be frustrated or seriously hindered.

4.0 Establishing Objectives

The areas of potential conflict arise where the objectives of society and the organisation are at variance with one another. The first step therefore is to identify both the objectives of society and those of the organisation. This process should indicate areas of acceptable risk and also the means to minimise the risks that have been identified.

4.1 Corporate Objectives

The corporate objectives of the organisation can be established firstly on general and then more specific levels. At the general level the company should establish the nature of the business in which they are engaged and the reason for their involvement in that particular field. Current objectives should be reviewed in the light of the activities which the company has identified are crucial to the long term development and survival of the company, given the current state of and expected developments in the technological, economic, political and social environments in which the company operates. Objectives therefore cannot be finally determined without thorough analysis of the impact of social and political factors upon the organisation.

At a more specific level, Ansoff in *Corporate Strategy* (Penguin) has identified a series of quantitative objectives, namely targets for

- growth in sales - if in fact this is a desired objective given market conditions and alternative opportunities available to the company;
- growth in market share;
- growth in earnings as a means of both providing resources for reinvestment and attracting fresh sources of capital;
- continuing development of new products and markets;
- continuing expansion of the company's customer population; and
- minimisation of seasonal or cyclical fluctuations in earnings and sales.

These generalised objectives are of course affected by factors internal to the company such as technology, the size of the productive unit and the existence or otherwise of economies of scale, the nature of the industry and the company's attitude to risk. The initial objectives are then modified in the light of the constraints or factors peculiar to the organisation concerned and a corporate commercial strategy formed. Only once these have been determined can the consideration of the effect of political and social variable be incorporated and analysed.

4.2 Political Objectives

The task of determining the objectives of society is of greater complexity due to the diversity of opinion that exists even within a mono-cultural society. Lloyd *(op cit)* suggests that a consideration of the political aspirations of the society as reflected by its respective political institutions is one approach to the problem. Such political objectives fall into two principal areas:

1) those about which there is at present little controversy between the shades of political opinion - i.e. the areas of common ground - such as the rights of the individual to privacy, to choose his government, not to be discriminated against on the grounds of sex, race, creed, disability etc, to equal treatment under the law, to the freedom of the press, etc as is the case in many western democracies. There are however variations in each nation state of which an organisation has to be aware. These objectives remain relatively fixed in the medium if not the long term and exist irrespective of the political opinions/beliefs of those in power.

2) those which are the subject of political controversy. In many cases these areas of difference may concern the means by which a commonly held goal should be achieved. For example the debate in the U.K. between the merits of public or social ownership on one hand and private ownership and the operation of the market on the other. These political pressures on the business enterprise are

therefore dependent on the government of the day; the anticipation and preparation for such changes being in turn dependent in forecasting the ongoing outcome of the political struggle.

4.2.1 Sources of information

In the U.K. a wide range of opportunities exist for political debate and discussion, providing the discerning observer with sufficient evidence from which to form a judgment about the issues on which there is a degree of consensus, those which are contentious and areas of potential change. Obviously these are bound to vary depending on the country involved but in general the main sources of such information are:

The Media
News and current affairs coverage is not restricted to the recording of facts but also the reporting of opinion. It follows therefore that the media is an important primary source of the climate of opinion within the country.

The manner, style and even content of the events and issues reported may also reveal the trend of opinion as the views of the reporter, the editor or the management of the organisation providing the service may influence the manner in which an article or report is written.

It should be noted that newspapers, radio and TV provide an important source of political or official opinion in societies where the authorities seek to influence opinion through the media by means of censorship or propaganda and should not be discounted on account of its bias.

In addition to reporting opinion the media also facilitates the expression of opinion by the public through the medium of letters to the editor, invitations to contribute articles, 'phone-ins' and audience participation.

Pressure groups.
Pressure groups in the U.K. number many thousands. Some are restricted to narrowly defined local issues while others like the TUC and CBI have a national forum. As the descriptor suggests they exist to articulate specific objectives, interests, ideas and values in the hope that their representations and arguments will influence the government's decision and policy-making process. They are distinguishable from political parties in that they do not present themselves as candidates for government and are concerned only with a particular issue or small range of issues. Their strategic importance is that of a catalyst for change as evidenced by the fact that many pressure group interests eventually become official political party policy and eventually legislation thereby establishing a cultural norm. In the U.K. the environmental/conservationist lobby has been successful in this respect.

Pressure groups seek to make their views known in a variety of ways. These include: **propaganda** such as the conduct of public meetings and advertising; **representation** where evidence to Royal Commissions, lobbying of Parliament, retention of MPs and direct communication with decision and policy-makers are among the tactics employed; and the **supply of information** perhaps to an MP if he has neither the time nor resources to gather it himself.

Political parties
Political parties in contrast to pressure groups address themselves to a wide range of issues of interest to the voter in an attempt to seek their support to allow them to fulfill their goal of the achievement of political power and form a government. Party policy is formulated by the party activists which then becomes either official party policy if approved at the official party conference or recommendations to the leadership, dependent on the constitution of the party concerned. Events and decisions at the party conference then become the most important indicators of the policies of the party for the incoming period as these policies form the platform on which representatives of the respective parties stand at general, by and municipal elections. Debate within the various parties is always taking place as new or revised policies are formulated. Some parties are less secretive than others about their differences at this stage so that new trends of political thought may be detected at an early stage in some instances.

Some caution has to be exercised in this regard as the views of party activists tend to be more extreme than those of the electorate. This has led David Butler to coin the term the *paradox of party difference,* as a means to summarise the situation that many party leaders and MPs find themselves in, namely pulled towards the extremes by activists and pulled towards the centre by the voters - a feature which becomes even more pronounced when the party is in opposition.

Royal Commission
From time to time a Royal Commission is instigated to consider particular problems confronting society. The Law Commission is one such body. The Commission takes opinion from interested parties and learned bodies, some of its findings ultimately making their way onto the statute books.

4.2.2 Identification of issues

Although the findings may be imprecise and incomplete, a review of these issues identifies areas upon which attention can be focused and the appropriate steps taken.

Lloyd *(op cit)* cites one example of political and social awareness, that of General Electric in the United States, and lists factors which had been identified at the time of the report as key issues for the future:

a) constraints on corporate growth ranging from national growth policy to policy on monopolies;

b) corporate accountability, including personal liability of managers and directors, board representatives and disclosure;

c) human resource management, including job enlargement and flexible scheduling;

d) constraint on employee relations from government, unions and other groups;

e) problems of business-government partnership in problem-solving;

f) growing government in business decision-making through consumerism, environmentalism, industrial reorganisation and inflation control.

5.0 Social Risks

Social stability - the ability of a society to accommodate, and possibly encourage, change in such a manner as to allow the benefits of change to be enjoyed by the population as a whole - is in the interest of business, government and populace alike. That this stability is dependent on the complex interrelationships between the economic, social and political environments makes prediction of the exact nature and direction of future change hazardous.

5.1 Factors for Social Instability

Whilst it may not be possible to predict accurately the outcome of the blend of the above forces it is necessary to identify those factors which may give rise to instability. Some which have been identified are:

a) 'insoluble' problems, such as chronic and continuing unemployment in Western Europe in the late 1970's and 1980's; inflation as in Germany of the 1920s and Argentina of the 1980s; and international indebtedness as in Brazil of the 1980s;

b) a parliamentary impasse preventing effective government thus generating conditions for dictatorship, military coup or revolution such as in Lebanon in the 1980s;

c) the growth of private violence and the breakdown of accepted authority;

d) the uneven growth of economic sectors such as the North/South divide in U.K. and Italy or the growing divergence between the industrialised and the third world;

e) racial or tribal conflicts or tensions such as in India prior to independence, Nigeria in the 1960s, Uganda in the 1970s and Northern Ireland throughout the twentieth century;

f) the alienation of the intelligentsia thus providing leadership for opposition groups such as in South Africa during the 1960s to the 1980s and the Philippines in the 1970s and 1980s;

g) humiliation in war such as Russia and Germany following the first world war and Argentina in 1983.

5.2 Indicators of Social Instability in the U.K.

Evidence for the factors which have been listed above can be determined from a number of social statistics. The adequacy of these measures is variable from country to country and in only a few cases are directly comparable. In the U.K. however, aspects of national and local life such as

- experience of unemployment, inflation, education and work;
- attitudes to unemployment, work, the environment, organised labour, racial, sexual or religious discrimination and law and order;
- the nature of the community - i.e. the age distribution of the population, whether it is urban, suburban or rural and its racial composition;
- the nature of the local economic infrastructure - i.e whether the population is skilled and whether these skills are currently being employed, the extent of educational provision, the degree of dependence of an area on a single company or industry for the maintenance of its economic and therefore social life etc, and
- the general economic situation and the position of a particular community relative to it.

are relatively well documented in official publications by the government departments, for example in the U.K., 'Social Trends' issued by the Central Statistical Office (CSO) and national opinion surveys which are regularly conducted and published.

For instance, in the area of employment, the highest areas of unemployment are concentrated in the 'traditional' industrial heartlands such as Strathclyde, the North East and Merseyside with rates in excess of 16%. This is reflected in the reduction of the numbers employed in the manufacturing industries which are largely concentrated in the above and other areas such as the Midlands together with the increase of the numbers employed in the service industries to 64% of the working population, many of which are located in the London and South East areas particularly as a result of the growth in the financial sector.

These changes have implications for the prosperity of the business organisation in terms of proximity to markets, the availability of staff, the cost of land, the impact on the local environment and the attitudes of the local community.

According to surveys of British opinion, the majority of the British population believe in the importance of work for the fulfillment of material, social and personal needs of self-worth and are therefore supportive of 'positive' government policy designed to alleviate the problem. Given the strength of this feeling, no U.K. government can afford to ignore this view, the differences between the parties being in the the policies adopted to meet these objectives. The implications for change as the result of a change in government are obvious.

The link between social and economic deprivation giving rise to poorer health, higher crime and other indicators is well documented in official statistics. The implications for disruption to production as the result of absenteeism and vandalism should be considered by the company. Furthermore corporate 'assets' have more recently been subject to new kinds of threats such as kidnapping or compromise of product integrity, sabotage by extremist pressure groups, developments which have not been unconnected with changes in both the manner in which opinion is formed and expressed and attitudes in society.

Social instability therefore is not only a matter for governments but also the organisations which seek to trade in the society affected.

Changes in the social environment need not be those that threaten the assets of the organisation for there to be a significant impact on its activities, as the following table, which identifies specific ways in which selected social issues influence the activities of business organisations, indicates:

ACTIVITY	SOCIAL ISSUE	EXAMPLES
Product design and characteristics	Safety, Use, Ecological impact	Drugs, toys, fire-arms, napalm, waste disposal, car fumes
Production processes	Occupational health and safety, Ecological impact	Mine safety, noise abatement, air and water pollution
Work force	Equal employment and other employment practices	Minority and female hiring, migrant labour
Marketing	Selling and advertising ethics, Consumer affairs	Restrictive practices, public acceptability and responsiveness

Table 9/1

As reflection on the above issues would indicate, experience in the U.K. shows that issues which may start as a the specific interest of a minority pressure group can eventually be transformed into cultural norms by the enactment of legislation.

In conclusion therefore the identification of trends in social and cultural development is necessary whether these indicate social instability or the alteration of the legislative environment within a stable social environment.

6.0 Political Risks

The most obvious area of interface with the political environment is in the field of government-business relations whether at local or government level. Government is usually acknowledged as the single most important determinant of corporate behaviour even within a market economy.

6.1 The Role of Government

Governments, irrespective of political affiliation are generally believed to assume responsibility for the following major areas of activity:

a) as representative of the people balancing power between organisations and the individual and increasingly between government and the individual through a system of laws and regulations in such areas as employment practices, pollution and market power;

b) the provision of services, particularly in the areas of social and economic infrastructure such as education, health, protection from fire, utilities, telecommunications and transport;

c) the consumption of a substantial proportion of a nation's Gross Domestic Product - government is a major consumer in the modern economy, active in most sectors of the economy, and crucial to the success of many companies which rely on government purchasing;

d) the management of industries such as coal, steel, gas and electricity. Obviously the extent of government involvement is dependent on the views of the political party in power;

e) the formulation of foreign policy;

f) economic management, concerned with the implementation of monetary and fiscal policies as a means of increasing the wealth and welfare of the nation.

Government is therefore involved with industry over a wide range of areas at both local and national levels. Nationally these would include:

- the imposition of minimum acceptable standards in such areas as pollution and quality controls;
- the provision of training and regulations of conditions at work;
- employee and product safety;
- pressures for greater employee participation in the decision-making that affects their lives;
- support for consumer movements through regulation of conditions of sale and trade description laws;
- taxation and incomes policy;
- the regulation of external relations with other countries through such things as tariff barriers, exchange control, discriminatory taxation or purchasing policies, export promotion subsidies, trade boycotts etc.

Since individual operating units are located within a specific community, these are affected by local conditions such as rate of local tax or level of rates and local government planning and building control policies. The impact of the organisation on the local community in terms of the economic and environmental profile of the area creates further points of contact and perhaps conflict.

As governments and social pressures change so too will the range, nature, and scope of the area of the government-business interface at local and national level. In these events forewarned is forearmed, so that the organisation which has acknowledged the existence of these tensions will be in a better position to move to reduce them as the situation demands, a strategy which requires a longer-term and wider world-view.

6.2 Political instability

Political change need not infer upheaval as the mark of political stability is the accommodation of change within existing national political institutions. Political change therefore will be a natural process reflecting changes and developments in society at large. If however these institutions are unable to sustain or accommodate change and reflect the movements and trends in society then conditions for political instability exist.

Political instability infers a new range of threat to those with which the organisation has to cope in a conventional situation. Again it is impossible to predict the effect of changes in the political arena but identification of the trends which give rise to such a situation provides a measure of protection. Some of the factors which have been identified are:

- strong internal factions;
- social unrest and disorder;
- recent or impending independence;
- new international alliances and relations with neighbouring countries;
- forthcoming elections;
- extreme programmes;
- vested interests of local business groups;
- proximity to armed conflict.

The manifestation of political instability can take a number of forms. In ascending order, these are often classified as social disorder, riots, civil war and revolution. The likelihood and severity of civil strife is frequently a function of two factors:

1) the level of 'perceived deprivation';
2) the methods employed by those in government to deal with the pressures created under a situation of perceived deprivation.

6.2.1 Perceived deprivation

This phrase is used to describe the difference between on one hand, the material standards and conditions of living that the citizens of the country justifiably believe themselves to be entitled to - their **value expectations,** and on the other the amount of these goods and conditions that they think they are able to get and keep - their **value capabilities.**

The higher the level of perceived deprivation the greater is the likelihood of civil strife. This however may be reduced by the fashion in which these forces are handled by those in power.

6.2.2 Methods of control

The relationship between those in government and those governed is crucial. The pressures referred to above will be exacerbated if the path of progress towards the fulfillment of the value expectations of the governed is denied to any part of the population with the necessary qualifications to realise these expectations. In addition the authority of government is dependent on its legitimacy in the eyes of the population at large. The position of government is therefore by no means assured and may lead to insecurity on the part of its members. The manner in which government deals with potential threats to its legitimacy, authority and therefore power is a further determinant in the level of civil strife.

A government faced with these pressures has two main courses of action open to it. Either it can take account of the voices calling for change and seek to accommodate these pressures within existing structures or it can attempt to repress these forces by means of the civil or military establishment.

6.3 Checklist

Due to the interrelationships between the political, and social environments threats arising from these areas are usually lumped together for the purposes of analysis. The following checklist, which is based on one devised by P Nagy in *Country Risk* (Euromoney), follows this trend.

Social disorders, riots civil war and revolution arise from the same underlying factors, the seriousness of the situation determining whether conditions of social disorder will deteriorate to a point of civil war or revolution. The checklist is in two parts:

1) a series of statements concerning the underlying factors which give rise to civil strife to which a yes/no response is required;

2) an indication of the degree or intensity to which the factors indicated apply.

Nagy in Country Risk: Euromoney Publications

Riots, disorders are possible if:

– there is a deep-seated or bitter antagonism between sections of the population because of:

		YES	NO
* ethnic			
* tribal			
* religious			
* ideological	differences		
* other (specify)			

....

....

– there is discontent or antagonism related to unequal income-distribution:

* between social classes
* between regions

– one section of the population claims to be oppressed by the rest, be it a:

* social class
* region
* tribe
* religious group
* other (specify)

....

....

– there exists a strong movement in favour of autonomy or separation

– there is widespread discontent for other reasons (specify)

....

....

The probability of riots and disorders and the possibility and probability of civil war or revolution depends on the following factors:

	VERY	FAIRLY	NOT AT ALL
– the tension, discontent, antagonism is high			

– the government is:

* weak (unable to control situation)
* unsuccessful in efforts (if any) to defuse the tension through appropriate reform

– the discontented groups are:

* vocal and/or
* well organized
* well armed
* led by able, fanatical, impulsive or irresponsible leaders
* effective support from abroad

Table 9/2

7.0 Summary

The principal thrust of this chapter has been to examine, albeit briefly, the nature of social and political environments and from the analysis derive certain measures or indicators which could be employed to identify trends within the current climate of political opinion and social and cultural development that will determine the future complexion of the social and political landscape. This is no easy matter as the cultural, economic and political forces of change within society are subtly and closely interrelated. Neither does the same model work for each society.

It was argued that the business organisation should seek to understand the social and political process on the grounds that in itself was a product of these forces and displayed the classical political characteristics of resource allocation, the exercise of authority and power and the reconciliation of competing interests, that the competitive behaviour of the business organisation was also a component of change in society, and that it was necessary element of corporate survival to understand both that change was occurring and the nature of that change.

As with all changes, those in the social and political environments provide both opportunities and pose threats. The threats arise from the points of tension between the firm and society. The tension it should be recalled by reference to figure 1/1 occurs where the objectives of the two parties clash. Thus it is necessary that these points of potential conflict be identified. Once identified the normal process of risk management can be applied and steps taken to either avoid the conflict of interest, reduce the shock of conflict - for example anticipating an area of difficulty and altering current practices to reduce the strength of an opposition's case - or prepare the organisation for the impact. These areas are identified by comparing the corporate objectives with those of society. It should be possible for corporate objectives to be specified clearly; the problem of discerning those of society is not as straightforward but can be determined by reference to the media of communication within the society and the areas of political agreement and controversy.

The analysis should not only reveal the trends within society but whether through its existing institutions it is able to accommodate change or if it is subject to instability. Whilst it is not possible to predict precisely the outcome of change it is possible to identify certain underlying factors which have been observed to give rise to social and political instability. Further information about these factors may be available in certain countries from sources such as national opinion surveys or official statistics about the level and distribution of income, the provision of educational opportunities, family expenditure, crime etc. These underlying factors can be incorporated in a checklist which can be used to determine their possibility and the probability of occurrence. Finally the manner in which the governing elite is elected and their authority legitimised and the means they adopt to solve areas of perceived deprivation suffered by their citizens are significant in determining the degree of seriousness of the impact of the factors leading to civil strife.

Chapter Ten

THE ORGANISATIONAL ENVIRONMENT

1.0 Introduction

The growth of organisations is closely linked with the development of the modern economy. Most modern organisations in the public or private sectors of the market economy date from the nineteenth century with much of the state apparatus of modern Britain only being able to trace its origins to the post 1945 period. These changes have been closely linked to economic development as the manufacturing process with the specialization and division of labour imposed new requirements on the organisation of the factors of production. The modern economy, whether based on market or centrally planned systems, is now one of organisations.

2.0 Key Points

The main purpose of this chapter is to

- identify the characteristics, objectives and functions of formal organisations;
- examine briefly the organisational function of risk management;
- explain and explore the uses and weaknesses of organisation charts and in particular their use to the risk manager;
- highlight the problems of bureaucratic organisations;
- document the role of the manager;
- discuss a number of management concepts and their relevance to risk management.

3.0 Organisations

The form of organisation referred to above which makes specific arrangements for the completion of particular tasks such as the manufacture of goods are described by organisational analysts as **formal organisations** to distinguish them from those **informal organisations** of family, friendship, community etc which have always existed but which lack the clearly defined goals and rules which characterize the formal organisation.

Formal organisations fall into two main categories, namely productive and non-productive. **Productive** organisations are those which provide goods and services for consumption, and includes those produced by the private sector such as furnishings, washing machines, banking, insurance etc and those provided by the state such as health and education. **Non-productive** organisations such as the church, the courts, trade unions etc are often linked with the institutional fabric of society which, whilst not providing an output in terms of goods or services, influence or control the behaviour of its citizens.

3.1 Characteristics of Organisations

It has already been noted that formal organisations are distinguished from informal organisation by the existence of goals and rules. Formal organisations also possess a number of other features:

- a **name** by which the organisation is known and often identified separately in law as in the case of a limited company;
- **rules** which govern the activities of the organisation. These may be written, verbal or assumed to be known and in some instances be imposed by law. For example rules regarding certain legal obligations of a limited company are contained in the Companies Acts.
- **goals** or **objectives** which the organisation seeks to achieve such as the pursuit of profit in the case of the business organisation. Care should be taken not to confuse the end with the means, for example the objective of ICI is to make profits, the means are the manufacture and sale of chemical and related products;
- **positions** or **roles** to fulfill within the organisation. Obviously smaller organisations will concentrate a number of these roles in one person;
- a chain of **authority** to enable the jobs and functions to be carried out;
- **power** and its delegation. Power is said to rest with those with the legal right to take decisions. This however is often delegated as in the case of a large public company where the power is delegated by the shareholders to senior management;
- **records** of their activities, which in some instances - eg tax collection - may be legally required.

3.2 Objectives

Organisations can be identified from their objectives. For instance the goals of nationalised industries, government, trade unions, political parties and others identify the nature of the activity and basis on which decisions are made. It has been said that the objective of the business organisations is the pursuit of profit. Generally speaking this is interpreted as referring to the criterion of the maximisation of profits through:

a) the production and supply of goods to markets in which demand has been identified as increasing;
b) the minimisation of the costs of production; and
c) limiting output to profit maximising levels that was considered in the section on the economic environment.

It should be noted that many business organisations may have goals which are subsidiary to this one such as standards of quality, after sales service, commitment to the community etc. These however are subsidiary to the principal one of the generation of profits.

The establishment of realistic and organisationally acceptable risk management objectives will require to bear this point in mind. As has been already indicated other objectives may be fixed which could be of guidance in the formulation of risk management goals but the overall goal of profit is the final court of appeal.

3.3 Organisational Functions

Business organisations realise the goal of the generation of profit through the sale of goods and services. This involves organisation of the purchase of inputs - the factors of production; the production process itself whereby the inputs are converted into goods and services; and the sale of the output. The nature of the input and production process depends on whether the industry is primary, secondary or tertiary but the functions are the same. In addition a number of other functions exist:

- **finance and accounting,** in order to document the costs and revenues incurred and because there is a time lapse between the purchase of the inputs and the sale of outputs;
- **transport and distribution;**
- **personnel management** which is required as soon a someone other than the owner starts to work in the organisation. The organisation has to be able to relate to individual employees and their elected representatives and also comply with the relevant statutory obligations;
- **law and public relations.** The objective of profit maximisation is constrained by the regulatory and social framework within which the organisation operates. The organisation therefore has to be aware of its legal and social obligations in order to prevent infringement of these thus creating a poor public image with inevitable repercussions for its competitive position;
- **development.** To grow businesses require to develop existing products and extend its product range, a requirement which infers both technical and economic development. Growth therefore implies the need to manage the development of the business in these areas and the effect that these changes have on the surrounding socio-economic environment.

These functions can be concentrated in one person or be allocated to a number of different individuals depending on the size of the organisation.

3.3.1 The risk management function

The above functions have been discussed individually for the purposes of identification, in practice they operate in concert to forward the objectives of the firm. Thus the normal activities of a business necessarily involve most of the above disciplines. For example the production function whilst employing principles from science and technology has

i) financial implications in terms of the finance of working capital and costing of the output;

ii) personnel implications in terms of the selection, remuneration and training of the operatives;

iii) legal implications in terms of compliance with Health and Safety regulations; and

iv) the product and the technology of production may have been the outcome of research and development expenditure.

In addition the design of the product and its packaging are likely to have been influenced by considerations of transport and distribution as well as returns from market research.

Pure risk is also present in many business activities. This has been recognised in a number of areas. Engineering for safety and security has developed to high standards; the impact of uncertainty has been analysed in a number of business-related disciplines such as decision theory, operational research, financial theory and psychological behavioural theory; and the insurance industry has successfully developed on the basis of its expertise in handling such risks for the rest of industry. In the past however each of these various disciplines have for the most part remained apart pursuing their own lines of enquiry and producing their own solutions for dealing with the problem of pure risk. And generally the business community has delegated the handling of pure risk to the insurance industry.

Insurance however is principally a financing tool. The proper management of pure risk requires more than the means to pay for it when it occurs. The risk management function therefore seeks to combine the separate approaches to the management of pure risk and integrate the various disciplines to tackle the central problem of the management of pure risk through the process of the identification, analysis, control and financing. The movement towards the recognition of risk management as a separate function has been facilitated by the recognition of the proportion of corporate revenues devoted to insurance and also the values subject to pure risk.

3.4 Organisation Charts

The traditional way of depicting the structure of organisations is to draw an organisational chart as in Figure 10/1.

Charts help to define organisational relationships but they are useful only as a static model of a dynamic process. The chart does not organise *per se*, it describes some of the organizational relationships. The structures depicted therefore exist for the achievement of objectives, which means that the chart is not the organisation although the organisation may at one point in time be depicted by a particular structure.

Beardshaw & Palfreman in The Organisation in its Environment: *Pitman*

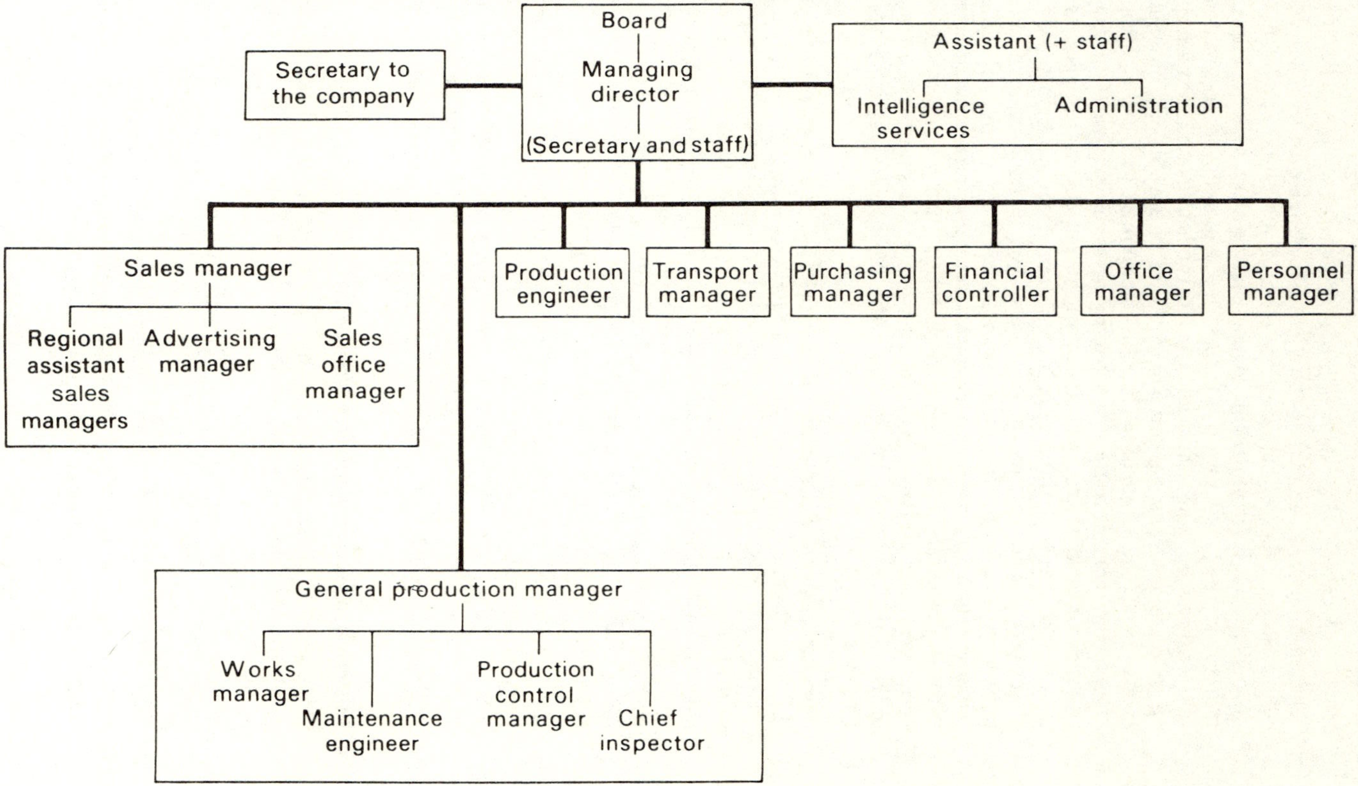

Fig. 10/1 : overview

The organisational chart depicts the formal structure, and shows that the relationships can be either **vertical** or **horizontal.** The vertical relationships indicate that the flow of communication should be both downwards - as directors and senior management seek to implement policy decisions, and upwards - necessary as a monitor of the effectiveness of the downward communication. The methods of communication should be selected carefully to complement the nature and purpose of the message sent, the length of the lines of communication and the personality of the receivers to ensure comprehension by the receiver. For example complex or lengthy instructions should be put in writing, such as in a manual, whereas shorter more urgent communication may be more effectively relayed by personal contact or telephone. Communication between people on the same organisational level but in different departments is referred to as horizontal communication, and is essential if the organisation is to act as a whole rather than a series of individual departments. Inter-departmental committees or the siting of departmental offices in close proximity are two means of encouraging this communication.

The static nature of the formal framework has led to the development of informal communication networks, otherwise known as the grapevine. These usually develop in clusters on a horizontal basis and relay information with exceptional speed. Properly used they complement the existing static organisational framework their dynamic nature permitting an organisation to react quickly to changing situations. The grapevine with its speed and flexibility should not be discouraged as decisions are more likely to be better informed and up-to-date. It also frees the formal channels for more 'critical' communication problems.

In the formal organisational structure, risk management has in the past been associated with either the accounting/finance or the company secretarial function. This picture has been confirmed by surveys carried out on the status of risk managers, the majority of whom report to the main board through the finance and accounting function.

3.5 Function of Organisational Structure

Organisation charts can serve a number of purposes. They show the structure of authority, power, responsibility and accountability, describe or chart the channels of communication and information flow, may be used to denote status and rank, define appropriate channels for appeals and assist in the task of identifying and relating the various parts of organisations.

3.5.1 Structure of authority, power, responsibility and accountability

Authority is the right which a manager has to make decisions within the scope of his own authority, assign tasks to subordinates (delegation) and request or require a satisfactory performance from subordinates. The extent to which the manager can enforce these rights depends on the measure of power available to him. **Power** is distinguished from authority because it is the ability rather than the right to do something. Therefore the manager's power is derived from his ability to promise or threaten or carry out his intention with respect to rewards or punishment. It is necessary to avoid conflict within the organisation that authority and power are balanced to ensure that a manager or any subordinate has the necessary power to enforce his authority and vice versa.

Authority derived from superiors is recognised formally, authority derived from subordinates on the basis of the beliefs of subordinates, the manager's personal character, his position or tradition is referred to as 'bottom-up' authority. This may be as equally powerful as the 'top-down' authority but does not feature in the formal chart.

Membership of the organisation confers **responsibility** upon each member to fulfill the function they have been called to perform. Responsibility is however the persons's obligation to himself to perform his tasks, i.e. the acceptance of the task creates the responsibility within the person. Responsibility therefore resides with the person which means that it does not flow through the organisation, as does authority, and that it **cannot** be delegated. Organisationally each member is accountable to his superior. **Accountability** exists because of a managers right to require satisfactory performance from his subordinates. Since a manager remains accountable to his superior for work delegated to him he **cannot** delegate accountability, even for work which he has delegated.

3.5.2 Communication and information flow

Without communication an organisation would never achieve coordinated, organised activities directed towards the fulfillment of its objectives. The organisation chart presents the plan or system defining the formal flow of information and communication within the organisation. Information is also necessary to the manager for the exercise of power and authority.

3.5.3 Status, rank and appeals

Whilst position on an organisation chart alone does not necessarily confer high rank or status it is an important indicator; and generally speaking the higher on the organisation the greater is the level of status and rank.

Since disagreements are inevitable in any complex organisation a well-defined and understood system for the resolution of conflicts is necessary. The hierarchical nature of the organisation chart defines the appropriate channels for appeals which normally allows for the referral of problems upwards through the organisational structure to the position where a manager has sufficient power and authority to provide a solution binding on the parties concerned.

3.5.4 Identification and design aid

The organisation chart is useful in identifying relationships between various parts of the organisation so that an individual manager is able to identify the position, function, superiors and subordinates of both himself and his colleagues and thus be able to establish his identity within the organisation.

The chart may also be used as a design tool as a statement of the relationships and activities that would be desired within the organisation. It is therefore a means of communicating changes in the organisational structure that may be required in the interests of efficiency or in the light of changing events.

3.6 Organisation Charts and Risk Management

Despite their weaknesses organisation charts can be of use to the risk manager in such areas as the identification of organisational relationships and the formal channels of communication, recognition of the implications in terms of authority and accountability of the relationship between risk management and other functions and designing changes in the organisational structure to implement risk management.

The identification of organisational relationships is the groundwork for the recognition of the formal channels of communication and exploration of the implications of the place of risk management with respect to other parts of the organisation. Communication it has been noted is a two way process. Policy, directives and authority flow downward while accountability flows upwards. Knowledge of the lines of communication is necessary to secure effective communication of the implications of risk management upon the operations and obligations of the other functions and departments within the organisation. Consideration has to be given to the effectiveness and appropriateness of the means of communication such as the statement of policy, the use of manuals, memos, circulars, personal visits and the place of training.

Knowledge of the lines of communication will allow the risk manager to determine the lines of reporting and therefore be able to access information pertinent to the risk management function. Inconsistencies in the manner and lines of reporting of matters relevant to the management of the pure risks can also be identified at this stage. It may become necessary to reorganise existing arrangements or instigate new lines to provide adequate and reliable information for the identification and control of risk. In view of the inter-disciplinary nature of the risk management function the risk manager should be alert to the benefits to be derived from the judicious use of the informal channels of communication.

Determination of the lines of communication also identifies the structure of authority, power and accountability within the organisation. The relationship of the risk management function to others can be fixed and the ensuing implications for the exercise of authority explored and expressed. It is recognised that both senior management support - i.e. 'top-down' authority - and 'bottom-up' authority, perhaps through the establishment of the credibility of risk management with other functions is essential to the successful execution of the risk management function. The overall place of risk management has to be clear in order to establish the nature and degree of accountability of other functions and departments to risk management. Inherent in the risk management philosophy is the belief that it is not the responsibility of the risk but the line manager and ultimately the production line operative. The reporting lines for the risk management function have to be drawn across departmental boundaries. These requisites may have implications for the position which risk management will fill in the organisation chart.

Finally if redesign of management reporting structures is required to ensure consistency both in terms of the manner and destination of the reports or to implement a full programme of risk management an organisation chart showing the relationships and activities that are required can be prepared and circulated to the rest of the organisation as a means of stating the organisational changes. It can be used as a point of reference to determine the extent to which actual behaviour has deviated from that prescribed by the formal chart and from which the necessary corrective behaviour can be deduced.

3.7 Bureaucratic Organisations

This form of leadership which characterises the leadership structure of many modern organisations was identified by Max Weber, a German sociologist who defined it as a situation where the officers of the organisation became divorced from the actual work of the organisation. The organisational structures and management techniques were determined without reference to specific leaders being based instead on the rules and regulations established by the organisation which determined the various functional areas of production, finance, sales, etc. and allocated duties to be fulfilled by those responsible for these areas within the organisation. The result was a rigid hierarchy, remuneration based on position rather than productivity and the obligation to follow organisational procedures which implied that knowledge of the rules was part of the job.

According to Weber's analysis bureaucratic organisations have the following characteristics:

- there is a high degree of **specialisation** of labour;
- **rational.** Functional areas and offices within these areas are rationally and clearly determined and defined; a hierarchy of authority is clearly established and positions in the organisation being described in detail with respect to duties, responsibilities, authority and place;
- **professional,** i.e. employment and the measurement of performance in the organisation is based on the ability to perform a job as prescribed by the organisation's rules;
- **impersonal.** Authority depends on placing in the organisational hierarchy, thus the acceptance of the authority and the person exercising it need not be the same;
- **autonomous.** Specialisation allows officials to develop a degree of competence in a particular area which makes it difficult for an outsider to question their decisions.

- **stability** of tenure, career progression, salary, pension and other benefits.

Despite certain weaknesses that are considered below the bureaucratic organisation has in contrast to other leadership forms potential for the superior achievement of organisational goals through provision for the delegation of authority, power being associated with position rather than individuals, provision for the perpetuation of the organisation through a line of succession and an orderly transfer of power.

Awareness of the problems which afflict bureaucratic organisations is necessary for the risk manager to effectively fulfill his role. The most common problems are:

- **avoiding responsibility** by various means ranging from making decisions 'by the book', questioning the reliability, accuracy etc. of information provided, by appeal to established custom and practice and by pretending problems do not exist;
- **spreading responsibility** by the use of committees. The constructive use of committees can be of benefit to the organisation as discussed below, but since they are an impersonal body their members can hide behind the anonymous persona, escaping responsibility and severely diminishing accountability;
- **hoarding authority** is the other extreme and occurs when an executive, who believes in his decision making prowess, abrogates additional unauthorised authority to himself often when another executive is failing to fulfill his responsibilities or by empire building;
- **delay of decisions.** In large-scale organisations timely decisions are as important as correct decisions. The bureaucratic structure tends to mitigate against quick decisions;
- **formalism and ritualism.** Since conformity to rules is valued in bureaucratic organisations, the rules may become more important than the achievement of the organisational goals;
- **sabotage,** normally initiated by subordinates, can take a number of forms, such as depriving a superior of essential information, overloading a superior with information or doing exactly as instructed by the supervisor but nothing more.

4.0 The Management of Organisations

Observation of management practice has revealed a number of concepts and principles that are of assistance to managers in the fulfillment of their organisational responsibilities.

4.1 The Role of the Manager

The role of a manager is one which has been recognised as including the following functions:

- **creating,** i.e. relating previously unrelated things as a means of solving organisational problems, long term planning, product development, devising new methods of control etc.;
- **planning** to determines the direction of the organisation in terms of objectives set and methods of accomplishment and coordinating its activities towards the agreed objectives. Planning involves the formulation of policy to meet the stated objectives and the implementation of these policies by means of the establishment of procedures and rules;
- **organising** which is concerned with developing ways of implementing the ideas developed in the creating and planning process by determining the specific activities that are necessary to accomplish the planned goals, grouping the activities into a logical pattern, framework or structure and assigning the activities to specific positions and people;
- **motivating,** by applying the insights afforded by studies into a) the determinants of human behaviour and b) the determinants of human behaviour in organisations in order to integrate the behaviour of the members with the interests of the organisation;
- **communicating.** The ability of mankind to communicate over time, distance, culture has enabled it to band together to achieve common objectives. Effective communication is therefore necessary if objectives, plans, policies are to be achieved. Its successful implementation is a function of, on one hand the manner and method chosen to 'transmit' the message, and on the other perception of the message which is conditioned by the experiences and environment of the recipients of the message;
- **controlling,** by monitoring the outcome of the actual events with plans and correcting deviations where necessary.

4.2 Line and Staff

The concept of line and staff is of use in structuring the tasks and relationships of an organisation. Care however has to be exercised in the use of the terms for they can apply to two distinctly different viewpoints. Firstly there is the view, often taken by a person from without the organisation, that line and staff denote different **functions** in the organisation. Line staff are perceived as those with direct responsibility for the accomplishment of the objectives of the enterprise. All other officials are staff. Secondly the other approach is that the terms refer to **authority** relationships, the viewpoint this time being from the person receiving the instructions, such that line managers have relatively unlimited authority over those to whom directions are given, whereas the authority of staff officials is restricted to their functional areas.

A major problem associated with this concept is that of potential conflict related to status within the organisation, line members being viewed as of greater importance and the staff personnel being rated as second-class members of the organisation. Much of the difficulty lies not in the contribution which is made by either section but in the measurement of the contribution, since that of the line members is more straightforward to gauge than that of the staff.

Within the terms set out above the risk manager would in most instances be categorised as staff. He however has to overcome the problem of status and gain the acceptance and support of line managers before any serious risk management can be accomplished within the enterprise. He must be aware that his advice and recommendations will be viewed by line managers, in the first instance, as of secondary importance. The significance of acquiring senior management support for risk management initiatives is obvious at this point.

4.3 Centralisation and Decentralisation

This concept refers to the degree of delegation of duties, power and authority to lower levels of an organisation or to the effective level of decision making for a particular area under consideration. Decentralisation is normally adopted when a greater degree of member participation is desired with the aim of securing higher commitment to organisational goals. When decentralisation is adopted and operating divisions are granted a degree of autonomy, their main responsibility becomes the generation of profits, with much of the reporting that would have been made to central management being devolved to the operating unit.

Centralisation is adopted when greater management control is required perhaps to ensure more effective integration of organisational activities. The growth of information technology and computerisation has increased the possibility of large organisations being managed effectively from the centre. This has reduced the pressure for decentralisation that many companies had been facing.

The practice of risk management must take account of the extent of decentralisation within the organisation. For example, it would be inappropriate for a highly centralised risk management approach to be implemented if a company's international operations were organised on an autonomous divisional basis. Access to the required information at each of the divisional units would be difficult from the centre, necessitating an alternative strategy more in keeping with the prevailing organisational arrangements, such as the appointment of risk management representatives in the separate locations on a functional basis with their activities being coordinated by the risk management advisor.

4.4 Committees

Committees as a means of bureaucratic sabotage have already been mentioned. They do however have a number of advantages, such as:

- the production of creative ideas;
- an effective means of transmitting information and ideas to interested organisational members and the coordination of activities;

- increased participation in decision making may lead to higher motivation;
- where no single manager has sufficient power and authority the committee may be a means of consolidating the power and authority of the respective functional managers and produce an authoritative decision for both functional areas;
- the abilities of a number of people are combined in committee either as a means of providing advice to a manager or for producing 'better' decisions.

Committees of course are open to criticisms on a number of grounds such as their cost, that they produce not better decisions but decisions either of the lowest common denominator or indecision, that they are subject to the tyranny of a minority, and that they are subject to abuse in terms of split accountability and as a means of avoiding action.

The main problem with a committee therefore is how to derive the maximum benefit from its use, a goal which requires an awareness of their problems and skillful leadership.

4.5 Span of Management

This concept refers to the number of persons and activities that a manager can effectively manage and is limited by his schedule, knowledge, personality, energy and other factors. This is of importance because as organisations grow their complexity, in terms of the number of organisational relationships, increases faster than the numerical growth. Given a certain pattern of relationships between a supervisor and two subordinates one writer has shown the following increase in the number of relationships:

Number of subordinates	Number of relationships
1	1
2	6
3	18
4	44
5	100
6	220
7	490
8	1080
9	2376
10	5210

Table 10/1

Whilst the method may be subject to some criticism, the conclusion of the rapid acceleration in the number of relationships is beyond doubt.

In practice the span of management can vary widely, but many writers have suggested that the number of direct subordinates should be kept in single figures. A relatively small or narrow span of management has limitations in terms of the additional costs and the added complexities of communication and coordination. Large or wide spans of management mean that a manager is unable to exercise direct control and supervision. This however may encourage initiative and development of subordinates as they are required to take decisions on their own. The reduced costs of fewer managers may be partially offset by the higher costs of higher-quality managers required for the larger jobs with greater independence and responsibility.

The span of management concept highlights the number of potential relationships that may occur as the risk manager's responsibility extends throughout the enterprise and reinforces the point that the risk manager alone cannot manage risk but must delegate this to managers of other functional areas.

5.0 Summary and Conclusion

This chapter has sought to examine the structure and management practice of modern organisations from the perspective of risk management. This has involved firstly, consideration of the importance of the principal goal of the business enterprise, namely that of profitability in the formulation of risk management policy; secondly, the relationship of risk management to the other functional areas such as production, sales, finance and accounting etc and the functional role which risk management plays in the business organisation; and thirdly, the information about organisational relationships that can be gleaned from an organisational chart, in particular those relating to the structure of authority and accountability and the channels of communication, and the insight that can be gained from such an analysis for the effective operation or implementation of a risk management strategy.

The potential pure risk implications of certain managerial concepts such as the distinction between line and staff, decentralisation and centralisation, committees and the span of management were also considered, as were the particular problems that have been encountered in the management of bureaucratic organisations with the purpose of providing a number of diagnostic tools of organisational breakdown. Awareness of the existence of such problems is also beneficial as to be forewarned is to be forearmed.

Chapter Eleven

THE ORGANISATION AND ITS ENVIRONMENT

1.0 Introduction

Organisations do not exist in a vacuum, but in association with their environment which provides their resources and imposes limitations on their activities. As the environment is constantly changing the organisation must adapt if it wishes to survive. As failure to perceive environmental changes is a prime cause of organisational failure it constitutes a primary pure risk to the organisation.

The elements of the environment are normally identified as those of physical resources, climate and location - comprising the natural environment; economic and market conditions, social, cultural, religious and political attitudes, legislation and the people who work and interact within the organisation which in this text have been described as the business environment. Recalling figure 1/1 it was noted that from time to time the firm would be required to manage the tensions and constraints that the interaction of these various forces would place on its operations as the clashes or collisions that occurred were the factors that gave rise to the incidence of pure risk. The role of the natural environment as a source of pure risk has already been well established, the part of the business environment is less clearly defined.

The following cases seek to illustrate different ways in which a working knowledge of the components of the business environment can apprise the risk manager of the wider implications of the pure risk problem.

2.0 Automotive Supplies PLC - the Economic Environment

Automotive Supplies are a West Midlands based company engaged in the manufacture and supply of components and accessories to the U.K. car industry. They currently operate from seven production units of similar size in terms of workforce, output and area, four of which are in the Midlands area. An effective risk management programme is in place covering the major areas of initial concern such as employee health and safety, security, fire, flood and environmental risks.

The technology and economics of the production process for a few of their products stipulates that certain manufacturing units concentrate on the production of a particular product, although not to the exclusion of all others. This accounts for the finding, following an analysis of the output of each unit, that 90% of all light bulb production originates from one factory located north of Manchester.

Investigation of the annual accounts for the past few years further reveals that approximately 55% of net profits are attributable to the manufacture and sale of light bulbs, with none of the other products contributing more than 10% to the remainder of the profits.

Automotive Supplies shares the light bulb market with three other major suppliers. Together they account for more than 85% of all sales. Recent economic conditions have meant that demand is just beginning to pick up with the result that there is still some excess capacity in the industry. This recovery of demand is also beginning to increase the presence of a number of large overseas competitors.

Economically speaking, the raison d'etre of any manufacturing plant is production as factors of production are employed solely for the output they can produce, implying that the most serious effect of any loss is the loss of production. The effect of any loss of production is determined by conditions in the market. A brief consideration of some of the economic aspects can help explain the current pattern of profitability and the ensuing threats to its continuation.

Some of these factors are:

– the conditions in the market.

The market conditions set out above are characteristic of those of an oligopolistic market. The features of the oligopolistic market discussed in chapter 3 section 3.4 but in brief are -:

- little or no price competition;
- firms acting together, whether formally or informally;
- ability to pass higher factor costs on to consumer;
- high barriers to entry such as advertising or set-up costs.

These features may help explain the dominance of bulb related profits in the company's annual figures as the conditions of competition are allowing the market participants to earn above 'normal' profits, this position being maintained by the existence of high barriers to entry. The following observations can be made:

i) the market conditions in the U.K. bulb market help account for their contribution to annual results assuming that other of the company's products do not compete under similar market conditions. The higher profitability in this market will mean that the impact of lost bulb production will be greater relative to losses in other products;

ii) this loss may be exacerbated by the current excess capacity in the market allowing competitors to expand production to meet the shortfall. This share of the market may not be recoverable;

iii) the vulnerability of the barriers to entry could determine whether a major production loss of one of the suppliers in the bulb market provides sufficient incentive to another producer, who need not be of U.K. origin, to move into the market;

iv) the terms of business in the market, i.e. long or short term contractual arrangements, will also affect the degree of loss suffered for example long term agreements will preserve the customer base at the price of increased costs to meet these commitments. Failure to do so will lead to fewer customers and may give rise to civil actions.

– the nature of the product.

The demand for all items produced by Automotive Supplies is a derived demand - i.e. it depends on the demand for motor vehicles. Events in the light bulb market are therefore dependent on those in the car market and, in particular, on the performance of the manufacturers they supply.

As conditions in the capital goods industries tend to be more volatile, the market share lost in an upswing of the market which will not be recoverable during the lifetime of the cycle will be greater than normal market conditions would presuppose. Given the circumstances described above, this is an accurate forecast of the results of lost production at the current time.

– external factors such as exchange rate movements and import penetration.

In the example it has been indicated that foreign competitors may be able to fill a production shortfall. This loss in market share would be extremely difficult to recover. If the competitor is already involved in the manufacture of similar products and is based in the EEC, the barriers to entry are not likely to be substantial.

Downward movements in the exchange rate make imports more expensive and therefore provide a measure of protection to domestic industry. Provided the movements lead to a realistic valuation of sterling in terms of such factors as level of U.K. interest rates, price levels and the balance of trade, the exchange rate is not a disadvantage to Automotive. The extent of exchange losses will depend on (a) the volatility of sterling; and (b) the proportion of imported raw materials in the final product.

3.0 MNC PLC - the Socio-political Environment

MNC PLC are a U.K.-based multinational corporation with worldwide sales, manufacturing capacity in Europe (including the U.K.), North America and an industrialising country in Asia, and a London Head Office. The London offices are those of the Group holding company. The Group operations are organised on a geographical basis with a substantial degree of autonomy being given to the various geographical centres. The core business of the Group and the principal subsidiaries is engineering with a further strategic number of subsidiaries in support and allied industries. The remainder comprise a heterogeneous group with little or no relation to the core business. The Group has been implementing a programme of phased withdrawal from these areas.

The problems of operating in differing social and political climates has been underlined by a number of recent events. A review of Group operations has identified that the following are particularly susceptible to threats emerging from the socio-political environment: production
premises
personnel
products
communications.

These threats can occur at any location, although some are more at risk than others to particular risks. The risks are deliberate in that they are the deliberate acts of persons which may or may not be specifically directed against the company.

The above review has designate the following areas as high-risk relative to other operational areas.

A. Non-U.K. European location

This country has a stable, democratically elected government which enjoys a broad measure of support from the community and the media, in particular in its approach to a significant terrorist problem.

The manufacturing unit is situated in a region which falls within the area of the terrorist activities and has suffered some attacks, the reasons for which have been cited as (a) the U.K. origin of the operating subsidiary and (b) the siting of a manufacturing unit in another country of which the terrorist group disapproves.

The threats have been predominately to personnel. An executive has been kidnapped in the past and more recently executives have been subject to harassment and intimidation.

The company, which is a major employer of local labour, has been encouraged by the government to retain production in the area to maintain the health and balance of the regional economy.

It is expected that attacks on personnel will continue to be the *modus operandi* of the terrorist group, but the possibility of attacks on premises or products cannot be ruled out.

B. Developing country location

A rapidly industrialising country in which the Group has had a presence for a number of years. The subsidiary in this country is of strategic importance to the Group as it is the production and distribution centre for the geographical area in which it is located.

The move to industrialisation which has produced significant changes in the social and domestic fabric of the country has taken place over a relatively short period of time which has resulted in a number of growing tensions.

Analysis of the social and political institutions has produced the following findings:

- a well developed educational system with literacy rates above average for the region and a number of centres of higher learning;
- a highly developed pre-industrialised indigenous culture;
- the presence of a sizeable middle class;
- a mixture of religions with high adherence rates;

- current method of government is a military dictatorship which overthrew a civilian dictatorship and introduced reforms leading to rapid industrialisation;
- government censorship of media;
- token power possessed by opposition parties;
- rapid increase in GNP but the benefits of industrialisation not experienced equally by population;
- a strong desire amongst middle and educated classes for movement towards greater democracy;
- a predominance of foreign multinational corporations in the industrial sector;
- support for peaceful political change from important foreign powers.

Pressure on the military dictatorship in the past had exacted promises of democratic elections 'in the future', but many of the educated classes are impatient with progress towards this target. The current rulers have been able to resist further pressure from this source because of the silence of the middle-classes.

The concern of the company is that if the growing pressure for change is not accommodated the ensuing riots and civil disorder may escalate to a position of civil strife. Such an outcome is possible because of the ability of the opposition leaders to organise effective resistance and the past record of the government in quelling opposition. The company is therefore under threat for a number of reasons including:

i) a general association with the process of industrialisation and the consequent loss of former way of life; and

ii) the general social and political tension produced by rapid change.

It is likely, given past experience of unrest in similar circumstances, that the aspects of the organisation most susceptible to the potential disorder are production, premises and communications.

The Group is understandably concerned about the developments over which it has no control affecting this strategic part of its operations. However an awareness of the factors which lead to political and social instability, as discussed in chapter 9, enables a more rational appraisal of the situation from which tentative conclusions can be drawn or more information sought.

4.0 Tandd Ltd - the Legal Environment

Tandd Ltd is the transport and distribution subsidiary of the Allied Industrial Group, an industrial conglomerate with production units in most regions of the U.K. and the EEC. Tandd provides transport and distribution services for both group and outside companies.

It has a network of depots which comprise facilities for warehousing, distribution and overnight parking of vehicles in a number of the major industrial centres of the U.K., some of which are located on industrial estates others being situated in urban areas. In recent years the business has expanded partly as a result of increased demand for its services and partly through a policy of selective acquisition of smaller local companies in the same field. The general expansion has prompted the company to to decide to upgrade and expand the facilities at most of these depots.

Part of the reason for the recent development of business has been a movement towards specialisation in the transportation of chemicals and related substances. To that end the company has been considering an enhancement of its current fleet by further investment in new tankers with larger capacity and additional safety features. As these developments represent a major investment of company resources the decision has been referred to the parent company for final approval.

In accord with normal company practice the matter has been referred to the risk management department for its comments, particularly in relation to insurance covers for the extended premises and the new tankers as these are arranged at group level. The risk manager has also been asked to consider the implications of the additional risks adopted by the use of the new larger tankers, the status of the safety features and the expansion of the existing depots.

Investigation of the above has indicated that the additional risks subsumed by the acquisition of the tankers fall within the bounds of acceptability and that the incorporation of the cost of security and fire protection systems already in existence at the depots will not jeopardize the viability of the investment.

However it has been found that to proceed at the moment would risk infringing the provisions of the Control of Industrial Major Accident Hazards (CIMA) Regulations - a Statutory Instrument issued under the Health and Safety at Work Act 1974. The enforcement of these regulations is the responsibility of the Health and Safety Executive (HSE) which would be able to bring its statutory powers to bear in the event of disregard of the regulations. The CIMA Regulations are directed at manufacturers who have control over certain dangerous substances and are engaged in certain 'industrial activities' as defined by the regulations.

The problem for the company is that calculations have revealed that the increased capacity of the tankers and warehouses together with the increased amount of chemicals falling within the definition of 'dangerous substance' have combined to breach the limits set by the regulations for the storage of dangerous substances. If the company wishes to proceed it will be required to:

i) inform the local HSE of the development;

ii) give three months notice of the intention to store certain substances on the site;

iii) prove to the satisfaction of the HSE that the major accident hazards have been identified and that appropriate measures for the prevention and/or control of the consequences of a major accident have been taken;

iv) prepare an on-site emergency plan and, in liaison with the local authority an off-site emergency plan which has to be regularly updated; and

v) inform, normally in conjunction with the local authority, those residing in the locality who are likely to be affected by any accident of: the nature of the hazard, the safety measures that have been taken and the correct behaviour that they should adopt in the event of an accident.

The investigation also revealed that weekly returns of the type and quantities of substances stored were made to the distribution manager, but this information was not reported to either the company secretary who had responsibility for the administrative aspects of insurance or the group risk management department.

The incident also identified a potential public relations problem in addition to the legal complications as a number of the depots were situated in urban areas, as previously mentioned. The case highlights other factors of relevance to the business environment. For instance the regulations, introduced in 1984, were based on an EEC directive which reflected growing social and political pressure to control the activities of manufacturers dealing with substances that could give rise to a major accident, particularly where the installations concerned were located close to centres of population.

5.0 Summary and Conclusion

Three examples of the relationship between the business environment and pure risk have been studied, each seeking to illustrate the additional insight that can be brought to the process of the identification and analysis of pure risk through an awareness of the constituent parts of the business environment. The necessarily arbitrary selection and division of the incidents that were related serves to underline that, in the real world, there are no such convenient divisions and that to exclude the elements of the business environment is to ignore a significant input to the outcome of any risk management decision.

INDEX